CW00394448

Mrs Slocombe's Bull at a Gate Cookery Book

I dedicate this book to:

Devon, its picturesque towns, inspirational
characters, and farming communities.

My mother and my late grandmothers, for passing on their knowledge
and giving me a great trip down memory lane whilst writing this.

My partner Chris Pedlar, aka 'Mr Slocombe', for actually
managing to keep up with me, coping with the chaos
in the kitchen, and clearing up my mess.

My son Zak for the surfer's slant to 'fish on a stick'.

My goofy Labradors that tried to con me into believing they could actually
cook. They couldn't by the way, but they still made fabulous kitchen
assistants and took their position on quality control very seriously.

And finally, ME (cos I've worked bloody hard on this!).

Special thanks to:

My publisher, Oliver Tooley, who's demonstrated the patience of a
saint and who's always been close to hand for my many queries.

My artist, Ian Shapland, a very talented chap
who also possesses 'saintly attributes'.

Thanks and 'hats off' (literally, ahem!) to Willie Thorne and Joe Pasquale
for being good sports and letting me give them a mention in this book too.

The Pasture-Fed Livestock Association for their ongoing commitment to
raising awareness of the importance of food, farming and environmental
impacts and seeking to find the best way forward for a harmonious future.

- - - - -

Just before going to print one of my goofy Labradors, MoMo,
passed away; she was 13 years old. A special thank you to her for
enhancing my life so much. MoMo, you were loved enormously,
and you are missed equally. Run free beautiful girl. X

Mrs Slocombe's Bull at a Gate Cookery Book

by

Tracey Slocombe

Copyright 2019 - Tracey Slocombe.
The right of Tracey Slocombe to be identified as
the author of this work is asserted.
No unauthorised copy may be made of any part or whole of this
book without written consent from the author Tracey Slocombe.
Recipes, images and stories used, with permission, in
this book remain the property of their
respective authors and may not be copied or used
without the original author's consent.
All the characters and scenarios in this book are real.
Mrs Slocombe notes: apart from my hooters; I told my
artist to be generous in that department!

First Edition Hardcover
ISBN : 978-1-911438-64-9

Contents

Introduction

Mrs Slocombe is incredibly passionate about food; she will give you a little bit more than some fabulous recipes. They are, of course, the core of this book but she will also send you on a nostalgia trip in Grandma's Kitchen, get you tipsy in Seven Drunken Nights, take you on a little jolly round the globe to explore some cuisines and use them for your next social gathering. Being an avid animal lover and doting on her two pet Labradors, Lady & Mo-Mo, she's even knocked up a treat for them.

Being a born and bred country bird and former beef farmer has provided Mrs S with a greater understanding about food, its production and of course the many ethical considerations that arise from it. I hate to say it, but food has become very political, and rightly so too. Greater transparency is available to us these days around our food and issues that arise from it, which in turn enable us to make informed choices with the way we source, shop and ultimately live. The way I see it is simple: respect what is on your plate, especially if it's meat. After all, an animal has lost its life to provide you with nutrition; do it some justice! When it comes to sourcing meat, get to know your butcher and don't be afraid to ask him questions about the origins of the meat you are about to buy. Any butcher who is worth dealing with will tell you proudly where his meat comes from, what breed it is, if it's been grass fed only (be aware of commonly used loopholes to claim grass fed only too; many claim this but in fact are fattened on grains for the last 6 months of their lives) and even provide you with an ear tag number giving 100% traceability.

I also have a notion of this: far too much food waste occurs too often. Look at what you can turn into a preserve or cook and freeze from your surplus fruit and veg.

Fussy eaters, that's me! I like things the way I like it, end of. I fast developed this notion of 'if you want anything doing right, do it yourself' years ago, after being so disgruntled every time I ate out, or bought a shop-made pork pie to find it was dry on the inside, bah! Couple that with the fact I live in the middle of nowhere and it's a bit of a jaunt to get a takeaway, the time it takes to get the Landy out, drive to town, queue and drive back to find it's the best part of the way to being cold and I would probably end up giving it to the dogs anyway. It's just as quick to roll up your sleeves and do it yourself. So, takeaway is something I rarely eat these days. I like it that way too, and I have a few select restaurants I go to when I do fancy a trough out.

Mrs S also likes to use food to raise awareness and funds for charitable concerns. My particular favourite was the Ginger Monty which occurred purely from goofing around with gingerbreads following an appearance on ITV's The All New Monty, when Chris Pedlar aka 'Mr Slocombe' got his kit off and literally bared all alongside some celebrities in aid of raising awareness of men's health. It ended up with him, Willie Thorne and Joe Pasquale being forever immortalised in dough. These little Montys proved quite a hit, Willie Thorne stating 'it's the best he's looked in years'. You'll never look at gingerbread in the same way again and no prizes for guessing what Mrs Slocombe's future contributions to these fund-raising coffee mornings are going to consist of!

Mrs S also spent much time chewing the cud, thinking of a way to keep you, the reader, entertained whilst your little creation is simmering on the stove top. So do look out for a few tales of banter along the way that will almost certainly bring a smile to your face.

Mrs S loves the area she lives in and couldn't help but get a bit creative in the kitchen to commemorate this, with creations of the Milton Damerel, the South Molten, Hartland's Tiddy, Teddy Toddy Pie, River Taw, Beef Torrington, and Ilfracombe Slammer! As well as focussing on this great place to reside, a few of the well-known folk were also rounded up to feature as well.

- Julian Seager – an actor and friend of mine living locally and known for his roles in *Death Race 4*, *Cursed*, *Fisherman's Friends*, *Poldark*, *Doc Martin*, and *Viking Legacy*. Mrs Slocombe creates him a mead fit for the modern-day Viking who's in a rush and lacks patience!
- Simon Dawson – radio presenter, writer, author and a proper 'good-lifer' gives me his beer bread recipe.
- Oliver Tooley – author, publisher, and sometime radio presenter, gives me his tongue in cheek contribution of Wok Aléatoire in the Seven Drunken Nights section.
- Johnny Kingdom – a true champion of everything Exmoor. A wildlife expert, filmmaker, and photographer. Sadly no longer with us, his widow Julie gives Mrs Slocombe his favourite recipe to create.
- Lynne Hall – founder of K9 Focus contributes Lickin' Lips Liver Cake, for the dogs of course, although the odd pussy is partial to these too!

Once Upon a Time

Once upon a time, Mrs Slocombe had an idea (she has far too many of these, usually met with a chorus of despairing sighs followed by, "Let me sit down first," from those around her!).

She wanted her own catering business (no biggy then!).

Unfazed and stomping in where angels fear to tread, the research process and plan of action began.

Mrs Slocombe knew it was going to involve beef as this was her field (pun intended!) and was seeking a signature beef dish which used UK native breed beef, high in Omega 3, full of flavour with the fats providing a pleasing buttery texture.

Further research would be needed.

Mrs Slocombe and Rui Gordo – Piri-Piri & Co

In 2014 Mrs Slocombe visited Portugal where she caught up with her old mate Rui Gordo, known as Roo.

Roo used to live in North Devon up until 2012 when he decided to go back to his native lands and start up his own business, Piri-Piri & Co, specialising in hot chilli oils, seasonings, bee-keeping, and his own version of Portuguese Fire Water! (Oh my!)

When it was time for Mrs Slocombe to return to the UK, she did so armed with a big box of Roo's very own creation – Piri-Piri Honey.

This honey was super awesome: sweet, with a big delayed 'hoof' to it, I heaved a load into a beef chilli con carne one evening, it was a hit all round.

Could this be the signature dish that I was in search of?

It was certainly worthy of further investigation.

The UK Chilli Cook-Off Adventure

Keen to get some more research done on this dish, I decided to enter the UK Chilli Cook-off held in Burnham-on-Sea, Somerset to see how it would be received.

Aware it wasn't a traditional chilli, but my own version, I wasn't much concerned about what the judges thought but the general public's opinion was of utmost importance.

On the day of the contest I roped my dear friend Lorna in, to give me a hand.

The contest was held outside in the streets which also incorporated a rather large food festival. Being a former resident of Burnham-on-Sea, I was aware of the street where we were to be situated.

We would endure full-on exposure from the sea front which would be fine if the weather was OK but I knew it would still be windy regardless.

I checked the weather forecast before I left Devon: high winds and torrential rain which was in for the day – typical!

Undeterred, I devised a coping strategy. Grabbing what was left from a roll of black silage sheet and

some bricks to weight the gazebo down I left for Somerset.

We arrived late, roads were shut off, we had to carry all our equipment from the car to the site, weather was against us.

Conditions were difficult to say the least and what's more, we were against the clock!

Fortunately, I share the same trait as the bull – determination!

With the dish created, voting commenced and finished...

Mrs Slocombe scooped a 1st in the public vote!

Stressed, cold, bedraggled and, quite frankly, looking like I most definitely felt, the local press couldn't have picked a worse time to turn up wanting a picture.

'Winging it' from my imminent collapse one last time I managed to compose my posture and smile (not sure it

wasn't more a grimace though) sweetly for the camera. Forgot about trying to tame the wild windswept locks though... They spoke volumes of the day I'd had!

Anyway, let's crack on with that recipe!

Sweet Chilli Beef Con Carne

Serves 6 – 8 prep/cook time appx 30 mins

Ingredients

- 1 kg moo mince (beef)
- 2 onions (diced
- 1 large red pepper (diced)
- 2 beef stock cubes
- 1 carton tomato passata
- 2 tbs sunflower oil
- 2 red chillies (sliced)
- 1 tsp cumin
- 2 tsp fenugreek seeds (soaked overnight)
- 1 tsp hot chilli powder
- 2 tsp marjoram
- 4 garlic cloves (crushed)
- 1 teaspoon garam masala
- 2 cans red kidney beans (drained)
- 2-3 tbsp piri-piri honey

Method

In a large lidded wok, heat the oil.

Add onions, pepper, chillies, garlic and brown off.

Add beef mince and turn up the heat.

Method cont.

Keep stirring until brown then add all the herbs and spices and fold in well.

Add crumbled stock cubes.

Add passata and kidney beans.

When a bubbling point is reached simmer for 20 mins at least.

On a low heat you can leave this dish to further infuse for an hour or two longer.

If it starts to dry in this time add a little water.

Serve with basmati rice, warm nachos, or baked potato.

This is also great served cold in a wrap.

Tips

Use native UK breed beef sourced from your local butcher; don't worry about it being lean, a bit of fat is good for texture and it's also high in omega 3.

If you can't find piri-piri honey, just use a clear runny honey and adjust the chilli input according to taste.

Coriander leaves are a fabulous finishing touch to this dish.

Freezes well if you have any leftovers.

The Trailer Scenario

Following the success of 1st in UKCC, I began my search for a mobile catering unit. I had it in my head I wanted a red-and-black theme running through it. Scrolling through the pages of eBay, I came across a black one, but it only had one picture and no description whatsoever; however it did have a phone number - great!

I called it and, oh my, you couldn't make this guy up! Before you read any further, I want you to imagine a thick Brummie accent, spoken very slowly, except for when he got excited about telling me something, then he upped the tempo. He punctuated nearly every sentence with the word 'like' pronounced 'loike' throughout.

"Alroight?" he says...

"Fine, thank you. Can I talk to you about the catering unit you have for sale?"

"Oh roight, yeah sure."

"How many feet is it in length and width?"

"Oh, I dunno, loike, cos oi've only got a small ruler and it's in centimetres. Oi'll have to ask me mate, loike."

"OK. Is it a single or twin axle?"

"I dunno what you mean. Oi'll have to ask me mate, loike."

By this time I was thinking this was a wind up. Assuming the chap could count I asked him, "Can you count the number of wheels on it so I can determine if it's a single or a twin axle?"

He came back, "O roight, there's four."

"OK. It's a twin."

Bearing in mind I would have to tow it back from Brum, if it turned out to be any good, I then proceeded to ask him, "What are the tyres like?"

His response was, "They're black 'n' round 'n' pumped up, loike."

By this time I was nearly howling with laughter and could barely get any more words out. I was like one of those Romans in the well-known scene from Monty Python's Life of Brian.

"Anyway," I asked him, "why are you selling it?"

"Well," he said, "I bought it for me girlfriend, loike, cos I thought she could earn a bit o' wedge at the weekends, loike, doin' car boot sales."

"Ok," I replied.

His tone then started getting a bit excitable and he went on, "But her won't do it, loike, and her keeps leaving me, loike."

I just about managed to wheeze/squeak the next question out through sucked in cheeks and trying to focus on my breathing, dreading the answer as soon as I'd uttered it.

"Why don't you do it then?"

"Cos I won't get no customers!" his tone still excitable.

Feeling a bit sorry for him now, as he appeared almost distressed, I asked him, "What makes you say that?"

"Cos OI'M BLACK!" was his response!

I was thinking, you're in a city that's very culturally diverse?! My shoulders were shaking, my head nearly banging on the table... He then went on to say, "Oh hey, I hope you can reverse, loike?"

I managed to squeak out the word, "Yes."

"Oh, that's good," he continued, "cos it's in me back garden loike. It's been there for a year! It ended up there by accident, loike, and oi've got it stuck. I was trying to get it down the lane, loike, but then I realised I can't reverse!"

He continued, "So oi'm glad you can reverse."

Already in my head I could hear his next sentence. He didn't let me down.

"Cos if you couldn't, I'd have to ask me mate, loike."

I really don't know how I managed to get the following words out but somehow I managed to ask him if he could email me some more pictures of the unit, knowing full-well his 'mate' was going to get roped in, again, 'loike!'

Obviously, as I lived in North Devon, I didn't want a wasted journey to Brum if it wasn't what I was looking for.

He responded, "Can you call back later? I can't foind a pen, loike, to take your email address, but oi'll get me mate to take some more pictures, loike and get him to send you them."

Knowing full well I couldn't possibly manage another conversation later and come across as coherent if his mate or mate(s) were there, with visions of Daft, Dumb and Dopey all stood there scratching their heads, I decided to text him my email address instead of risking a call... I never did get a response nor did I ever receive any more pictures of the unit. I expect it is still stuck in his back garden... loike.

Johnny Kingdom

Man and Spirit of Exmoor

This book would be somehow incomplete without mentioning Johnny Kingdom, one of Exmoor's great characters, sadly no longer with us.

Over his many years filming on the wonderful landscape of Exmoor, he provided a huge amount of knowledge and valuable insight on wildlife, through his films.

When JK first started out on this pathway his equipment was only basic, but it allowed him to make films and show them in his local village halls, which led to him making videos for a living.

His dedication to this cause acknowledged no boundaries. He would often spend hours and days at a time lying in one spot or up a tree just to bring us that rare clip of rutting stags, playful foxes, badgers, and a myriad of birds.

JK was very much a sociable chap and enjoyed his gatherings whether that was in his local pub or having a picnic with his family on Exmoor.

In memory of this true countryman, his widow Julie has given Mrs Slocombe the recipe for her late husband's favourite teatime treat, a boiled fruit cake, to recreate.

I intend to make this one myself again, in October, during rutting season when I will take a slab of it on Exmoor in an attempt to catch a glimpse of some stags fighting for the hinds.

As you would always say JK, "Make sure the wind is in your face to avoid them catching your scent."

If you haven't read his books or seen any of his films I can thoroughly recommend

them; so many of the characters in his books I can relate to as I was brought up around folk like that.

It explains a lot, I'll just leave that there.

I hope you approve Mr Kingdom...

Julie Kingdom's Boiled Fruit Cake

Ingredients

- 4oz margarine
- 1 level tsp mixed spice
- 1 tsp bicarbonate of soda
- 2 mugs mixed fruit
- 2 mugs self raising flour
- 1 egg
- ¾ mug brown or white sugar
- 1 mug water
- Whole cherries (optional)

Method

Melt margarine in a pan with fruit, water, mixed spice, sugar, and bicarbonate of soda.

Boil together for a few minutes.

Wait to cool for a while.

Add egg, flour and whole cherries, stir and place in an 8" lined tin.

Cook at 150°C for 1¼ hours.

Nature's Free Foods

This section covers some of nature's free foods with recipes to make the best use of them. You will also find further on through the book some more recipes they can be used in.

Please only pick what you need; remember you are sharing with wildlife too. Avoid picking near a roadside and also after heavy rainfall because of pollutants. Always wash your pickings thoroughly before use.

If you're going on private land, please make sure you have the owner's permission and follow the country code. Thanks!

PS I will admit to never trying the deep-fried daisies as I've never been that desperately hungry!

Please note: With any form of foraging, please make sure you know what you're picking.

Ensure it hasn't been sprayed with any harmful chemicals.

If you're unsure what you're eating, seek advice where necessary...

Mrs Slocombe does not want to hear tales of the family pussy turning into a dragon, there being an ogre sat at the table where your husband used to sit, or of anyone being snuffed out!

Daisies – Deep-fried!

Ingredients

- 20-30 ox eye daisy flowers (with stems)
- 100g plain flour
- Pinch of bicarbonate of soda
- Appx 60ml ginger beer (lemonade or fizzy water can also be used instead)
- Herbs & spices are an optional extra
- A deep fryer for frying

Method

Preheat the deep fat fryer.

In a bowl, place flour and bicarb and mix.

Add a little of the ginger beer at a time to the mix whilst whisking.

You want to end up with a thick batter like consistency.

If you want to add some herbs and spices to the batter mix, do so now.

Holding onto the stem, dip the flower heads into the batter mix then straight into the fryer, repeat until all are used.

Remove when they have turned golden and place on some kitchen towel to drain any excess oil.

Serve as a side with some dips, add to a rocket salad for some texture.

For a sweet nibble lightly roll the flower head on a saucer of cinnamon and sugar as soon as it comes out the fryer.

Daisies are great to use as a decoration on your cakes or in a fruit infused drink.

Sloes

A fruit from the blackthorn, difficult to find on the moors but can be found on the fringes in hedgerows.

Great for wine making and sloe gin.

Picking time is usually around Oct/Nov.

Sloe Gin

Ingredients

- 500g sloes
- 250g caster sugar
- 1 litre gin

Method

Wash the sloes and prick them all over with a clean pin.

Place in a sterilised jar with the sugar and gin and give it a good shake up.

Leave the lid tightly on and shake the jar every day for the first week, reducing to every other day for the second week and then reduce it to once a week.

I like to let sloes infuse for 6 months but it can be used after appx 3 months.

Blackberries

Blackberry bushes can be found all over the UK.

At the risk of stating the obvious, the fruits are black when ripe.

They are best picked in August and September but not in October.

According to legend the devil tiddles on them in that month...

Not that the old wives' tale has ever deterred me.

When they're ripe they're ripe and if I want a blackberry pie or a bramble jelly they're getting picked!

Bramble Jelly recipe in Mrs Slocombe's Pantry.

Seaweed

This gift from the ocean has many uses in food from soups, salads, fish cakes and even breads.

Having said that, some seaweeds are not edible (a few even produce sulphuric acid) and therefore I recommend you check in a reputable foraging guide before trying this particular culinary treat!

Care should be taken when harvesting for seaweed. Never yank it up from the root but cut up far enough to allow new growth.

Avoid picking seaweed from a beach near a town, where there is sewage run off or near industrial sites.

Seaweed picking is best avoided in the summer. The best time for picking is between November and May.

Once you have collected your seaweed and taken it home, wash it and leave it to drip dry either over the bath, on the washing line or at a low temperature in an oven.

Don't leave the seaweed to soak in water for a long spell as you will end up with a bucket of slime!

You will need to ensure the seaweed is thoroughly dried before it is stored away. So long as it is kept completely dry it can be stored for a year or more.

If you notice over time a fine white powder growing on the seaweed, it's nothing to worry about, it's just the salt escaping.

Nettles

Nettle Tea

There are many claims made for the health benefits of stinging nettles. They are said to be good for easing sciatica, joint pain even reducing the size of an enlarged prostate amongst other ailments although there is little in the way of medical evidence to back this.

Speaking from personal experience, I know it worked for my sciatica.

Warning – can cause allergic reaction and mild stomach upset in some people.

Always seek professional advice if unsure, especially if you are allergy sensitive.

Use gloves for picking!

Ingredients

- 1 part nettles to 4 parts water (nip off leaves with as little as the stem as possible on them)
- Honey or sugar to sweeten

Method

Wash nettles in warm water in a saucepan.

Boil the amount of water needed for the quantity of nettles you are using.

1 cup of nettles needs 4 cups of water.

Place nettles in the boiling water and simmer for 15 mins.

Pour into cups and add honey or sugar to sweeten.

Elderberries

Elderberries are available in August, September and October.

Care should be taken when using. Avoid using the leaves, roots and bark as these contain harmful chemicals (lectin and cyanide) albeit in small quantities.

The berries also contain cyanide; however, cooking removes this.

There are several varieties of elderberry but the safe ones to use are the American and European elderberry.

It has been suggested elderberry contains many health benefits.

A great antioxidant, rich in vitamin C, fibre, anti-cancer, anti-diabetes and anti-inflammatory effects. (However, I cannot vouch for the veracity of these claims).

Use for jams, syrups, crumbles and chutney.

It is also well known for its use in making elderberry wine, and the flowers, of course, are used in elderflower cordial.

Note

The scientific name for Elder is Sambucus, but despite having the same name, the Italian drink Sambuca is not required to contain any elderberry.

Now, speaking of alcohol... read on.

Seven Drunken Nights

Well, there's many a time I've travelled across the country's moors....

Ahh, memories...

When I think of the West Country; its quaint pubs full of character and filled with colourful characters.

Overflowing with comical folk type music as well as the common folklore tales...

Well, I thought I would include a few creations and concoctions that involved alcohol.

Many and often a good time is had when such delights are shared in convivial company.

Mead (Fit For a Viking!)

This mead is so easy to make.

Ideal for the modern-day Viking who is in a rush.

It can be ready in just 6 weeks!

You can add different flavours if you want to change the ones listed below.

This was created for Julian Seager using his favourite flavours at his request.

I think he likes it!

Ingredients

- 1 gallon of spring water (warm)
- 1 packet of wine yeast
- 2 cups strawberries (quartered)
- 4 cinnamon sticks
- 4 cloves
- Handful sultanas
- 1.5kg honey
- 1-gallon demijohn
- Fermentation lock
- Sanitizing liquid/powder

Method

You will need to make sure that anything which is coming into contact with the mead is clear of bacteria.

So soak all your equipment* in the sanitizer (follow packet instructions) and leave it to dry naturally.

*Just to be clear; that's the equipment you'll be using to make the mead. What you choose do to keep any other 'equipment' clean is entirely up to you!

Warm half the water in a pan, add the honey and stir until dissolved.

Funnel into the demijohn, add fruits, spices and top up with the remaining water.

You will need to wait until the temperature of the liquid in the demijohn is below 90°F before adding the yeast because

if it's too warm, it will kill the yeast.

After you have dumped the yeast in the demijohn, you will need to shake the bejeezus* out of it for 5 mins constantly to aerate it.

*This is a technical cooking term which just means shake it very vigorously.

Don't forget to put the lid on!

Change the caps and put in the air lock (half filled with water). Make sure you have a tight seal.

You will notice a foam start to form within anything from a few hours to 36 hours.

Your demijohn will now need to be kept at room temperature, out of direct sunlight.

After 6 weeks, your mead is ready to be racked.

Don't forget to sterilise your equipment as before.

Farmer's Punch!

There's nothing like a cooling citrus number to unwind with after a long hot dusty day in the fields. Sit back, reflect, relax with nature, and admire your day's work.

Ingredients

(Probably serves just 1)

- ½ bottle pale ale
- Shot (or 2) of rum
- 350 ml Orange juice
- 1 tbsp honey
- 1 inch ginger
- Lime (sliced)
- Lemon (sliced
- Orange (sliced)
- Mint sprig
- Ice

Method

Place a slice each of the lemon, orange and lime, plus the ginger and mint sprig into a cocktail shaker (or equivalent).

Using a muddler, pestle, or the end of your rolling pin (whatever!) squash it all down ensuring you work out all those citrus juices and those oils from the ginger.

Add ice, honey, orange juice and rum then give it a good shake.

Add the pale ale and give it a much more gentle shake.

Strain into a pitcher, adding more ice if required.

Boozy Peaches

A Dessert and a Cocktail in One!

Ingredients

- 4 peaches (halved, sliced and chopped)
- 200g sugar
- 250mil water
- ¼ tsp grated nutmeg
- 1 tbsp dark brown sugar
- 1 slice of lemon
- 50ml brandy
- 2 tbsp chopped nuts
- Ice cream or cream to serve
- Lemonade or ginger beer (to top up for a cocktail)

Method

Dessert

Place water and sugar into a pan, bring to a boil stirring frequently.

Allow to cool.

Bung the lemon and some of the chopped peaches into a cocktail shaker and squash it down to release some colour and get the juice from the lemon.

Add sugar syrup and brandy to the shaker and shake well.

Place the remaining peaches in a bowl,

strain the liquid over the top and sprinkle with nutmeg.

Chill in the fridge for a few hours or overnight.

Just before serving, place the peach halves and brown sugar onto a hot griddle and lightly char to your liking.

Serve the peaches in dishes spooning some of the juices over the top with a sprinkle of chopped nuts.

Cocktail

It seems a shame to waste the leftover juice so you could turn it into a cocktail.

Place any leftovers back into the cocktail shaker, add a tad more brandy and top up with lemonade or ginger beer; both work well.

Give a gentle shake, pour over ice, decorate, and serve.

If you use ginger beer, rub the rim of the glass with some fresh root ginger for a little tingle & zing, just in case you didn't top up with enough brandy.

River Taw

This River Taw cocktail reminds me so much of the real McCoy; the colour after a good storm, the way it sits in a wide brimmed glass replicating the way the river sinks deep through the valleys it is travelling through.

This sociable river is joined by many and meets many on its journey from the fringes of Dartmoor to the fringes of Exmoor.

Ingredients

- 50ml chocolate liqueur
- 50ml whisky
- 100ml condensed milk
- Crunchy peanut butter
- Chocolate curls
- Chocolate sauce
- Ice

Method

Mix liqueur, whisky, and milk, then chill. (Chill the ingredients, not you. You still have work to do.)

Spread the peanut butter on a small plate so it's ½ an inch deep and dip the rim of the glass in the peanut butter.

Place the chocolate curls on another plate and roll the rim of the glass around so they stick to the peanut butter.

When you are ready to serve the cocktails, swirl a layer of chocolate sauce around the bottom half of the glass and then add your chilled liqueur.

Ilfracombe Slammer!

With a nod to a certain tall, imposing bronze lady who has caused considerable controversy since her arrival in Ilfracombe, I present a bold, shimmering controversy served in a tall imposing glass.

The red combined with glittering gold is reminiscent of one of the magnificent Devon sunsets you may be lucky enough to witness while drinking it.

One thing the West Country can be proud of is its fantastic ciders and you can pick your favourite one to go into this cocktail.

As for controversy? If the TRUTH be known, if you sink enough of this drink you won't give two hoots as to what's standing on the pier.

(Publisher's note: pleashe drink reshponshibly!)

Ingredients

- 200ml cider
- 200ml cranberry juice
- 25 ml whisky
- 25ml grenadine
- 4 cherries
- ½ tsp edible gold glitter

Method

Place cherries in the shaker and squash.

Add the rest of the ingredients to the shaker and give it a really good hammering!

Pour into a tall glass and give it a quick stir.

Sit back, enjoy the views, and sparkle!

Watermelon, Raspberry & Vodka Smoothie

Ingredients (makes 4 tumblers)

- 1 watermelon (flesh only puréed)
- 1 small cup vodka
- ½ cup of grenadine
- Handful of raspberries
- ½ cup of lemon juice
- 4 teaspoons of sugar
- Ice

Method

Nice easy one.

Heave all the ingredients in a large pitcher.

Plop the raspberries in and fold them in.

Chill in the fridge for a few hours and serve over ice!

Hot Cider Punch

This cider is great as a winter warmer for any outdoor feasts you may have planned or at a summer BBQ or just sat bubbling away on top of the Aga or wood burner on a cold winter's evening as you sit with your feet up reading a book.

This super-duper recipe is so easy and quick you can always make more if the suggested 2 litres isn't big enough for your party size.

Ingredients

- 2 litres of a good quality medium local cider
- 2 inches of fresh grated ginger (don't be tempted to use dried)
- 2 tablespoons of caster sugar
- ½ fresh orange sliced

Method

Nice and simple; just heave all the cider, sugar, orange and ginger into a saucepan, stir, cover and bring to the boil.

Make sure the lid is in situ as it will evaporate quite quickly.

Simmer for a few minutes.

It's done!

Use a soup ladle to transfer to some mugs.

If you want to give this number a little more 'hoof' try adding a drop of rum.

Simon Dawson's Beer Bread

Simon will be familiar to many, in North Devon and beyond, for his regular appearances on The Voice North Devon radio, and also several TV appearances on shows like *Countryfile* and Ben Fogle's *New Lives in the Wild*. Along with his wife Debbie he runs Hidden Valley Farm in Barbrook on Exmoor National Park, where he rears pigs and a host of other animals most of which are stark raving bonkers, but you'll have to get hold of his books (see back pages) to find out more about that.

Ingredients

- 250g strong bread flour
- 200g rye flour
- 14g (2 x sachets) dried yeast
- 1 x beer (330ml)
- Water if needed

Method

In a bowl, add rye flour, yeast, and beer. Mix well.

Cover with cling film and leave for 4 - 6 hours.

Add the bread flour and salt and mix until combined.

If the mix is a little dry, add a little water; too wet, add a little more flour. This bread is very forgiving like that.

Knead well for around 15 mins.

Cover and set to one side to rise.

Knock back, shape, and place in a loaf tin, leave to rise again for 1½ hours.

Preheat the oven to 220°C and bake for 10 minutes, then reduce the heat to 180°C and bake for a further 30 minutes.

(Adjust temp. lower for a fan oven).

It's important to bake this on a falling heat.

Drunken Cooking with Olli!

Oliver Tooley has lived in North Devon since 2011; came here for the quiet life, stayed for the people!

He is an author, publisher, sometime radio presenter, and father of four (it's OK, he says, he knows what's been causing it now!)

Olli has contributed his favourite drunken creation. (Mrs Slocombe is currently sourcing a drink awareness course for him!).

Cuisine Au Wok Aléatoire! By Oliver Tooley

We've all arrived home a bit drunk after being talked into a 'swift half' after work, haven't we? That first 'half' turns into a pint because you just don't have the strength of character to bold-faced ask for a half pint when faced with the friendly barperson, and then of course, you're embarrassed to leave before buying your round and before you know where you are you're doing the zig-zag walk home, passing up on the obvious curry because it's still a week until payday, until you arrive home absolutely ravenous.

This is where a creative approach to cookery is essential. You need to cook whatever you can find in the kitchen and somehow not end up with something that tastes like it was dredged up from a blocked drain. It doesn't matter if it LOOKS like it, just so long as it doesn't taste like it. When you're drunk, you're hungry enough to eat almost anything, but you're not an idiot.

Ingredients

• Random food items - see method.

Method

Preparation time: 5 minutes.

Longer if you have to go to the shops ... or A&E.

Cooking time: 15 – 20 minutes

Find a wok or large saucepan. Hopefully it is somewhere sensible like the dishwasher or next to the sink, although it might be in the living room or on the floor somewhere. If you can't find it on the first attempt, try moving some dirty laundry or empty food packaging to see if it's under there. Once you've found it and given it a good scrub to get rid of the burnt remains from yesterday's food, stick on the hob on a high heat; you're good to go.

Have a good look in all the food cupboards, the fridge and the freezer. Remember, the freezer is your friend. Unlike the fridge, most of the food here will be relatively fur free, and unlike the cupboard the packaging will be easy to get into. At this point it would be a good idea to add some oil to the wok. Be careful when you do this because the wok will be red hot now having been on a high heat with nothing in it while you were looking for food. The safest method is to stand on tiptoes and hold the oil bottle at arm's length, so that any splashback will just land safely on the floor.

Publisher's Note:

We take no responsibility should you actually follow any of these instructions.

As the smoke fills the kitchen, wedge a broom handle against the smoke alarm and toss in some chopped onion. If you're cooking raw meat, e.g. bacon, sausages, chicken or whatever, this should go in now. Try to make sure none of the packaging goes into the wok. As the meat and onions begin to burn, think about adding some moisture. Baked beans are a good bet if you can still operate a can opener. Alternatively try adding things like courgettes, cherry tomatoes, frozen mushrooms, peas, sweetcorn etc, or whatever you've got knocking about.

It's probably still burning a bit so add a glass of water and tomato puree, or some leftover wine, or beer, and stir rapidly. This is also the time to add any seasonings such as ketchup, brown sauce, sweet chilli sauce, soy sauce, etc. Once everything looks more or less brown and it starts bubbling, plate it up and wash up a fork.

A little tip for plating up, try to make sure all the food goes on the plate. You get extra points for not having sauce all over the edge.

Enjoy! (Then pass out!)

Cider and Sage Jelly

Ingredients

- 1130ml (2 pints) sweet local cider
- 1.5kg sugar
- 1 bottle of liquid pectin
- 2 - 4 heaped tbsp of dried sage (add according to taste)
- Suitable sterilised jars

Serving suggestion – great as an alternative to apple sauce to serve with pork, sausages, cheese and crackers.

Method

Put the cider and sugar in a large saucepan and mix well.

On a medium heat, warm gently until the sugar has dissolved, stirring frequently.

Add sage at the point all the sugar has dissolved.

Boil for a few mins, stirring regularly.

Add the liquid pectin and boil for a further 2 mins.

To check the jelly will set, remove a teaspoonful of the liquid from the pan and place on a chilled saucer. If a skin forms it's ready to be put in the jars; if it doesn't, it needs to be boiled for a tad longer.

Skim the pot and transfer the hot jelly into jars.

Screw on lids immediately to seal while still hot.

When cooled, store at room temperature.

It will keep for 6 months unopened at room temperature.

Mrs Slocombe's Pantry

Bramble Jelly

For me, there is nothing more satisfying than opening my pantry doors to pots of bramble jelly; it's like memories from a season have been captured in a jar. I love this on thick buttery toast but don't just stop at that, it's fabulous with chicken, pork, and cheese too!

Ingredients

- 1.4kg freshly picked blackberries (washed)
- 1.5kg sugar
- 150ml water
- Juice of 1 lemon
- 1 bottle of liquid pectin
- Sterilised jars
- Jelly bag and tripod stand

Method

Place fruit in a pan with water, bring to the boil and simmer until the fruits are soft.

Arrange jelly bag over a large bowl.

Tip the entire contents of the pan in the jelly bag and allow to drain; this may have to be done in stages depending on the size of the bag. You want to leave it draining for several hours.

If the liquid you are left with doesn't make 2 pints, make it up to 2 pints by adding water.

Add this back to the pan with sugar and lemon juice, and heat until the sugar has dissolved. Bring the pan to a rolling boil for 2 mins. Add the liquid pectin and continue boiling for a further 2 mins, stirring occasionally.

As a test to make sure the jelly will set, remove a teaspoon of the liquid and pour on a saucer; if it's ready, after a few minutes a skin will form on it.

Remove from heat and skim.

Pour into the jars whilst still hot; allow the jelly to cool and set before lidding.

Cucumber Pickles

Ingredients

- 2 cucumbers (cut length ways)
- 300ml white wine vinegar
- 2 tbsp sugar
- 2 tbsp black peppercorns
- 1 red chilli (de-seeded and finely chopped)
- 3 bay leaves

Method

Pack the cucumber slices tightly into a sterilised jar (or jars).

Heat up the vinegar, sugar and spices and boil for 3 mins.

Allow to cool slightly before pouring over the cucumber.

Lid and store.

Tip

These pickled cucumber slices are quick and easy to make.

Gives an added bit of zing to smoked fish, a topping for tuna or your beef burger (see page 54).

Caramel Fudge

Ingredients

- 450g demerara sugar
- 400ml double cream
- 50g unsalted butter
- 1 tbsp liquid glucose
- 3 teaspoons caramel essence
- Jam thermometer

Method

Line an 8x8 inch square tin with greaseproof paper.

Place all the ingredients (except essence) in a deep saucepan as you will need to allow room for the fudge to bubble up during the cooking process.

Put the pan on a medium to high heat and clip the thermometer to the side of the pan so it is submerged.

Stir all the time and scrape the bottom of the pan on a regular basis.

Tip

This is a great treat and fab to give away as presents at Christmas.

I usually make a big batch of this and freeze some.

Here I have made a caramel flavour but feel free to try other flavours too; mint and choc work well as does rum and raisin.

Increase the heat as necessary until it reaches a temperature of 116°C.

When this temperature has been reached, remove from heat and allow it to stand until it drops down to 110°C, then add the essence.

Using a hand mixer on a slow speed, start to whisk the fudge.

Increase the speed slowly and reduce the speed when the fudge has thickened considerably and has a matt appearance.

Keep whisking on a slow speed until the mixture reaches 60°C; this will stop any crystallisation as it cools.

Pour the mix into the tin and leave to set overnight at room temperature.

Proper Pickled Onions

Ingredients

- 1kg small shallots (peeled)
- 100g salt
- 400ml malt vinegar
- 400ml cider vinegar
- 100g sugar
- 2 packets pickling spice
- 3 red chillies (finely chopped)
- Optional extras (because they do look nice in the jars) are bay leaves and thyme sprigs.
- Sterilised jars

Tip

They're fantastic roasted too!

These classic pickled onions were a firm favourite from my grandma and are a regular feature in my pantry today. I prefer these when they are a year old: dark, strong, and full of flavour.

You don't have to wait that long for them though; you can tap into them after a month or so. Once you've made your own you will be unlikely to want shop bought ones again!

Method

Peel shallots removing the first layer also as this can be a bit tough.

Place shallots in a bowl and sprinkle with salt; shake them about a bit to ensure each gets a coating of salt.

Leave overnight in the fridge.

Remove shallots from the fridge, place in a colander and give them a rinse in cold water.

Leave to drain and dry.

In a saucepan, place vinegars, sugar, chillies and spices.

Put on a medium heat, bring to the boil, turn heat down and simmer for a few mins.

Remove pan from heat.

Place all the shallots into the jars, packing them in tight. Pour the vinegar mix into each jar and fill to the top. Seal and store.

Farmer's Pickle

Ingredients (sauce)

- 280g dark brown sugar
- 3 tbsp black treacle
- 1 teaspoon salt
- 4 tomatoes
- 2 tbsp lemon juice
- 4 tomatoes (quartered)
- 1 tsp crushed cloves
- 1 tsp cinnamon
- 1 tsp nutmeg
- 1 tsp paprika
- 1 tsp pepper
- 4 garlic cloves (minced)
- 550ml malt vinegar

Vegetable content

- 300g carrots (diced)
- 300g swede (diced)
- 1 small cauliflower (diced)
- 1 apple (diced)
- 1 onion (diced)
- 100g sultanas
- 2 tbsp cornflour

Method

Place all sauce ingredients into a large pan and bring to the boil stirring frequently until the sugar has dissolved.

Simmer for 20 mins.

Add the sauce to the mixed vegetables, bring back to the boil, cover and simmer for appx 1½ hours or until the veg is cooked to your liking.

Mix a little water with the cornflour and add at the end, just returning to the heat for a few mins to allow it to thicken.

Fill sterilised jars with the pickle and allow to infuse for at least 3 weeks.

Enjoy with your favourite cheddar or with bubble and squeak

Tip

Never eat cheddar straight from the fridge; always allow it to sit at room temperature for an hour.

Ring Ripper - Sweet Chilli Relish

Ingredients

- 1kg red peppers (roughly chopped)
- 100g red bird eye chillies (stalks removed, leave the seeds in)
- 50g red jalapeños
- 2 inches fresh ginger (peeled)
- 6 garlic cloves (peeled)
- 450g sugar
- 350ml white wine vinegar
- 2 tbsp balsamic vinegar
- Appx 6 sterilised bottles or jars

Method

Place peppers, chillies, ginger and garlic in a food processor and whiz up until it resembles a purée.

In a large saucepan, place vinegars, sugar and the purée and put on a high heat, stirring all the time until the sugar has dissolved.

Bring to a rolling boil, cover and simmer for appx 20 mins or until the mixture has thickened.

Spoon or funnel into the warm jars, ensuring each jar is nearly full to the brim, and screw the lid on firmly.

Tip

Great added to a stir fry, used as a marinade, a dip with warm nachos or drizzled over your favourite sandwich.

Pickled Sweet Chilli Beets

Ingredients

- 1kg beetroot (try different colours and sizes if you want to add some contrast to the jars)
- 600ml red wine vinegar
- 100ml orange juice (fresh)
- 100g sugar
- 4-6 red and or green chillies (2 sliced, leave the seeds in for an extra kick)
- Pickling spice
- Fresh bay leaves
- Sterilised jars

Method

Place the beets in a pan of lightly salted water and bring to the boil.

Simmer for appx 30 mins.

Drain and leave until cool enough to handle then peel the beets by gently rubbing the skins off.

Cut into quarters or slices and arrange snugly into jars.

In a pan place the rest of the ingredients.

Bring to the boil stirring often until the sugar has dissolved.

Simmer for 3 mins.

Allow to cool slightly before pouring the mix into the jars ensuring total coverage of the beets.

Lid and allow to infuse.

Tomato & Apple Chutney

Ingredients

- 1kg tomatoes (chopped)
- 1kg apples (peeled and chopped)
- 2 large onions (chopped)
- 2 cloves garlic (crushed)
- 100g sultanas
- 250g sugar
- 1 tbsp salt
- 560ml red wine vinegar
- 50ml balsamic vinegar
- 6-8 sterilised medium sized jars

Method

Heave all the ingredients into a large pan and stir well.

Slowly bring the pan to the boil stirring all the time until the sugar has dissolved.

Once boiling point has been reached, turn down the heat and simmer gently for 30 – 40 mins or until fruit is tender and chutney has thickened.

Whilst still hot, transfer to warm sterilised jars and seal.

Tip

Great with chicken wings or cheese and warm bread.

Indian Chutney

Ingredients

- 450g apples (peeled and chopped)
- 2 red peppers (diced)
- 225g sultanas
- 2 red chillies (chopped)
- 2 garlic cloves (crushed)
- 500ml red wine vinegar
- 80ml balsamic vinegar
- 450g soft brown sugar
- 1 teaspoon ground ginger
- 4 teaspoons curry powder
- 4 - 6 sterilised jars

Method

Place vinegars and sugar in a large saucepan.

Heat gently until the sugar has dissolved.

Add the rest of the ingredients to the pan and bring to a simmer stirring frequently.

Simmer for appx 30 mins or until the chutney has become thick and fruits have softened.

Pour into warm jars and seal.

Tip

This warming little creation is great with cold meats, roasted vegetables and cheeses.

Feasts for a Gathering!

It could be suggested food is used to create social cohesion around the globe so I thought I would take a little jolly around the world to bring you this next section. This is great for when you host a group gathering and want to create a taste sensation from all over the place.

If the group members each create a recipe or two from this following section to contribute to the platter.

There are many great things about North Devon and Exmoor to experience from the great food available from independent one-off shops, farmers' markets and pannier markets in the quaint little towns.

If you want to experience a bit of history there are several large manor houses available for hire across the region to host your gathering.

Their grandeur will leave you in awe even if they can appear somewhat intimidating from the exterior.

I will never forget the first time I walked into Buckland House located in Shebbear. I actually felt the history as soon as I walked through the doors. It really was like stepping back in time, provoking many thoughts as to how many servants had traipsed up and down those very corridors with the original thick, wonky slate floors I was now walking on. How many cooks from the bygones

had created fabulous feasts for that huge table I was about to serve lunch on?

The portion sizes in the following recipes have been devised around serving eight people, the notion being that everyone will sample a little of each dish.

Apart from the churros!

Jamaica

Marinated Jerk Chicken

Ingredients

- 8 chicken wings/ portions
- Juice of 1 lime
- ½ cup of coriander (chopped)
- 1 Scotch bonnet chilli (chopped finely)
- 3 tbsp of jerk seasoning
- 4 tbsp of rapeseed oil
- 2 tbsp of soy sauce
- 4 tbsp pineapple juice
- Splash of dark rum

Method

Combine all the above (apart from the chicken) in a bowl.

Arrange the chicken wings in an ovenproof dish.

Pour the marinade all over the chicken and use a pastry brush or equivalent to brush the mix all over the chicken pieces ensuring each bit gets a good covering.

Cover the dish in cling film and refrigerate for 8 hours or overnight.

Remove chicken from the fridge and leave to come up to room temperature for an hour.

Place in a preheated oven on a moderate-high heat (190°C) and roast for appx 40 - 45 mins.

Use any juice left from the dish to spoon over the chicken when serving.

Classic Jamaican Rice & Peas

Ingredients (serves 8)

- 300g basmati rice
- 300ml water
- 400g kidney beans (drained if using tinned or soaked and cooked if using dry)
- 150ml coconut cream
- ½ Scotch bonnet (chopped)
- 2 garlic cloves (chopped)
- ½ tsp ground pepper
- 1 tsp salt
- 1 tsp thyme (chopped)
- 1 tbsp desiccated coconut

Method

Bung everything except kidney beans in a large saucepan.

Bring to the boil and simmer slowly for appx 8 mins.

Add the kidney beans near the end of the cooking time

to heat through.

Tip

This is an absolute mainstay of Caribbean cuisine and, by the way, includes pretty much all the essential nutrients you need for a healthy diet.

It is also a great dish served hot or cold.

Caribbean Salsa

Ingredients

- 2 whole pineapples
- 2 red onions (sliced)
- 1 bell pepper or equivalent (sliced)
- ½ cup fresh coriander (chopped)
- 1 jalapeño (finely chopped)
- 1 lime
- Nachos for serving

Method

Cut the tops off the pineapples and cut around just inside the skin to remove the flesh as complete as you can.

Use a spray oil to give a light coating to the items for the grill prior to cooking.

Slice the pineapple into rings and grill until lightly charred and soft.

Repeat this with the onion slices and pepper.

When cool enough to handle, finely dice the lot and add to a bowl.

Mix in the jalapeño and coriander with a good squeeze of lime juice.

Stuff all the ingredients back in the pineapple skin and chill for a few hours before serving

USA

Tennessee Caramelised Burger

Despite the USA having a very multicultural style of cuisine, it's undeniable they LOVE their burgers!

In fact, many will say it's where the burger originated.

So, here I have created a giant burger for sharing using UK native breed beef, pasture fed only with a homemade burger bun to sit it in.

Serves 8 as part of a sharing platter

The Bun

Ingredients

- 500g strong white bread flour
- 1 tsp salt
- 1 tsp caster sugar
- 15g of unsalted butter or rapeseed oil
- 1 x 7g packet of fast action yeast.
- 300ml tepid water
- Sesame seeds to top
- 1 egg, beaten

Method

In a large bowl, place flour, yeast, salt, and sugar.

Make sure the yeast and salt don't touch each other at this stage as they really don't get on!

I keep them as far apart as possible on opposite sides of the bowl.

Yeast and sugar get on really well though, so I put the sugar on top of the yeast.

Now they have taken their safe positions you can mix them all together.

Using a dough hook attachment on an electric mixer, slowly add the melted butter/oil then the water whilst mixing at the same time.

Once the dough has been formed remove from the bowl and knead it for around 15 mins.

If the dough feels slightly wet, you will want to knead it on a floured surface.

When I knead, I have several techniques ranging from a massage to a punch and the occasional stretch and never in any consistent order.

Once the bread has been worked, roughly shape the dough and place in a non-stick lightly floured 10-inch cake tin.

Cover the tin with a clean tea towel and leave to rise in a warm room for appx 1 hour.

When the hour is up, brush the beaten egg on the top and sprinkle on the sesame seeds.

Place in a preheated oven 210°C fan/230°C/gas 8. Let it stay on a high heat for 15 mins then reduce the oven temp

down by appx 30°C for the last 15/20 mins.

Check the bread by tapping it; it will sound hollow when ready.

The Patty

Ingredients

- 1kg good quality beef mince
- 1-2 large onion (puréed)
- 1 large red chilli (finely chopped or just heave it in the food processor when you purée the onion).
- 2 cloves garlic (same as onion and chilli)
- 2-3 heaped tbsp cornflour
- Salt & pepper to season
- 2 tbsp caster sugar
- Good splosh of bourbon/whisky

Method

Mix the mince, onions, chilli, garlic and seasoning together in a large bowl until combined.

Add the cornflour and combine again.

In a 10-inch non-stick loose bottomed cake tin (I used the same pan I used to make the bread in to ensure the same size) place the beef mince in and firm it down evenly.

You will have to be quite savage, pushing it all down to ensure it sticks together and doesn't fall apart.

Place in the fridge for a few hours to chill.

Preheat the oven to a moderate heat and put the cake tin on a baking sheet to catch any drips and bake for appx 1 hour.

Check the patty for readiness by inserting a knife in the centre and pulling it apart slightly to make sure it's not still pink in the middle.

Place the patty in a large lightly oiled frying pan on a high heat.

Sprinkle the sugar on and around it and add the bourbon.

Caution – if using a real flame from gas hob, this will ignite so remove pan from the heat at the point of adding the bourbon, tilt the juices in the pan away from you, add bourbon and place back on the flame.

If you want the flame effect but are using an electric hob this can still be achieved by lighting the liquid using a long lighter at arm's length.

For the Dressing

- 4-6 rashers of smoked back bacon (cooked just before serving)
- Beef tomato (sliced)
- Gruyère cheese (thinly sliced)
- 5 or 6 chopped gherkins
- Lettuce
- Mayo
- Tomato ketchup

Continue frying for a couple of mins after the flames have died down.

Your burger is now ready to be dressed up and finished off.

Slice bread across and, starting from the bottom, drizzle a generous helping of mayonnaise and ketchup.

Arrange the lettuce leaves and tomato (I like to lightly grill my tomato first), bacon, burger, cheese and gherkins. (See cucumber pickle recipe on page 41)

Place under a hot grill to melt the cheese and put the top part of the bun on.

Cut into segments and serve immediately.

Japan
Teriyaki Glazed Ribs

Ingredients

- 1 rack pork ribs (allow 1-2 ribs per person)
- Rapeseed oil
- 3 tsp Chinese 5-spice
- Salt & pepper (just a dash of each)

Glaze

- 70ml soy sauce
- 60ml hoisin sauce
- Juice of ½ a fresh grapefruit
- 1 tbsp clear honey
- 70ml rice vinegar
- 1 chilli (de-seeded and finely chopped)
- 2 garlic cloves (crushed)
- 1 inch of root ginger (crushed)

Garnish

- 1-2 tbsp sesame seeds (toasted)
- Fresh coriander
- Spring onion or fresh chives (finely chopped)

Method

Make a rub for the ribs by mixing the Chinese 5 spice, salt and pepper.

Apply rub and wrap the ribs in foil as pork tends to dry out quickly

Place the ribs on a roasting tray and slow cook in the oven for 2 hours over a low heat.

Whilst that is cooking make the glaze.

After the ribs have been cooking for appx 45 mins, brush on some of the glaze and return to the oven.

Repeat this process again a couple more times.

When the final glaze is applied place under a hot grill for a few mins to char.

Served with a garnish of sesame seeds and spring onions.

Oriental Style Salad

This is a great one served cold or straight away.

Ingredients (serves 8)

- 4 nests of noodles
- Handful mange-tout (thinly sliced)
- 1 small carrot (shaved)
- 1 small red pepper (thinly sliced)
- 1 spring onion (thinly sliced
- 70ml soy sauce

Dressing

- 30ml hoisin sauce
- 2 tablespoons peanut butter
- Juice of 1 lime
- 70ml sesame oil
- 1 inch of fresh ginger
- 1 chilli
- Rice vinegar (60ml)

Method

Add the noodles to boiling water and cook for 3 mins.

As soon as cooked, drain and stir through some of the sesame oil to stop them sticking together.

When cold add the soy sauce and stir again.

Place all the ingredients for the dressing in a food processor and give it a good whiz up to make a runny paste like consistency.

Stir this through the noodles along with the mange-tout, carrot, onion and pepper.

Eat straight away or chill it in the fridge for a few hours.

Italy

Deep Pan Pesto & Mozzarella Pizza

Ingredients for the Pesto

- 3 tbsp pine nuts
- 3 garlic cloves
- 2 tbsp fresh grated parmesan
- Good sized bunch of basil (save some leaves for decorating the pizza, they do crisp up nicely too)
- Olive oil (add enough until your desired consistency is achieved, usually 4-8 tbsps)

Ingredients for the Pizza Base

- 400g plain flour
- 1 sachet of fast action yeast (7g)
- 1 tsp salt
- 1 tsp sugar
- 4 tbsp olive oil
- 220ml tepid water
- 1 tbsp cornmeal
- 2-3 cups grated mozzarella

Method for the Pesto

Toast the pine nuts in a dry pan until they turn slightly brown; keep them moving and don't let them burn!

Pound the pine nuts in a pestle and mortar as though they jilted you at the altar.

Crush the garlic and roughly chop the basil.

Add the olive oil and mix until you achieve the desired consistency: a thick paste.

Alternatively just bung everything in a blender and blitz it together.

It doesn't keep long so, if there's any left, bung it in the fridge and use within a day or two at most.

Method for the Base

Put the dry ingredients into a bowl and mix.

Add oil and water to the centre and mix using the dough hooks on an electric mixer.

Lightly flour a surface, turn out dough and knead for a few minutes.

Leave the dough to rest for 20 mins under a clean tea towel.

Roll and shape the pizza into a round shape.

Spread the pesto on the base and sprinkle the cheese on.

Use the basil leaves you kept back to decorate the edge and centre of the pizza.

Set the oven to maximum and allow it to get really hot before putting the pizza in.

This time waiting for the oven to get up to temperature will also give the dough a chance to rise a bit more.

Bake on high for appx 20 mins.

This is great served with some warm vine ripened tomatoes or the tomato and basil salad on page 144.

China

Shredded Crispy Beef

Ingredients

- 1 x 8oz rump steak (cut into matchstick thin strips)
- 4 tbsp cornflour
- Splash of milk
- 1 egg (beaten)
- Pinch Chinese 5-spice
- Salt & pepper
- Oil for frying

To serve

- Baby lettuce cups
- Red onion (thinly sliced)
- Sweet chilli sauce

Method

Place cornflour, spice and a dash of salt and pepper into a bowl. Combine with the egg and milk until the consistency of single cream is obtained.

Heat the oil either in a deep wok or fryer.

Toss all the strips of beef into the batter mix and coat evenly.

Depending on the size of your fryer/wok place a coated strip of beef in the oil one at a time, don't put too many in at once or they will all stick together in a clump.

Fry until golden in colour and agitate occasionally to stop them sticking together.

Drain each batch on kitchen paper and serve in the lettuce cups topped with the onion and a drizzling of sweet chilli sauce.

My Ring Ripper relish goes very well with this, see page 45.

Indonesia
Baby Corn and Satay Dip

Ingredients

Serves 8

- 16 baby corn
- 1 small onion (finely chopped)
- 2 tbsp crunchy peanut butter
- 1 tbsp sweet chilli sauce
- 1 tbsp soy sauce
- Water
- Oil for frying

Method

Lightly stir fry the corn in a large wok and set to one side.

In the same wok, add more oil if necessary, add the onion and lightly fry until soft.

Add the peanut butter, soy, chilli sauce and enough water until you reach a consistency you are happy with.

Heat for a few mins.

Serve in a ramekin dish with your corn for dipping.

Spain

Churros

Warning – You might want to make LOTS of these little Spanish sweet treats, incredibly moreish and simple to make. Great served on their own after rolling each one in a cinnamon and sugar mix and or with dips such as a warm melted chocolate, raspberry coulis, salted caramel and butterscotch.

This recipe makes approx 75 pieces.

Ingredients

- 225g plain flour
- 75g unsalted butter
- 675ml water
- 100g sugar
- ½ tsp salt
- 3 eggs
- Piping bag with a star nozzle or similar
- Oil for frying
- Sugar and cinnamon for rolling the churros in

Method

Put the water, sugar, butter, and salt into a large saucepan, bring it to the boil and immediately remove from the heat.

Add the flour and mix together (use a hand whisk as it's easier with a larger quantity like this).

Leave the mix to one side to cool before adding the eggs.

If the eggs are added when the mix is still hot they will start to cook; you don't want this to happen.

Put the oil on to heat on a medium setting.

Add the eggs to the mix and whisk again until it's all combined.

Put some of the mix into the piping bag ready for frying.

When the oil is hot enough start piping the churros in the oil one at a time, making each one appx 10cm in length.

When the churros are a nice golden-brown colour, they're ready to be removed from the oil.

Drain and place on a piece of kitchen paper to remove any excess oil before rolling in the sugar and cinnamon mix.

Repeat the process until all the mix is used.

These are best served warm so keep them in a warm oven until the rest have all been cooked.

Mrs Slocombe's Favourite Ways to Cook Meat

This section covers the many varied ways to cook meats from roasting, slow cooking, spit roasting, hot smoking and sous vide.

Pork

Whole Hog Roasting

See lamb spit roasting section on page 86

Roasted Belly Pork Slices

A great cheaper cut to have mid-week or even on a
Sunday with a melt in the mouth crackling.

Ingredients

- Belly pork slices (if a big joint is used, increase cooking time according to weight)
- Sea salt
- Black pepper

Method

Dry the pork slices with paper towel.

Score the skin and rub in the salt and season lightly with black pepper.

Place on a lightly oiled baking tray leaving a gap between each one.

Bake on a moderately high heat for an hour turning over once halfway through cooking.

Always ensure it is piping hot and the juices run clear.

If, like me, you prefer the crackling well done to the point of being slightly charred, here's how to avoid over cooking the slices:

simply cut the meat off when cooked, wrap in foil and leave on the side to keep warm.

Put the crackling back in the oven at the hottest point and turn the heat up full whack.

A further 10 mins like this will give you a perfect melt in the mouth crackling that won't break your gnashers!

Tip

Great served with Mrs Slocombe's Cider and Sage Jelly! See page 38.

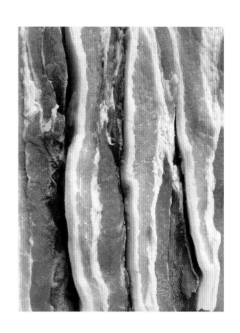

Candied Bacon

Candied bacon is so easy to make and is great served in a grape and fig salad (see page 145).

Either smash it up when cooked and use it as sprinkles or leave the rashers whole, great added to mashed potatoes and mashed eggs too!

Ingredients

- Smoked streaky bacon
- Maple syrup
- Oil

Method

Lightly grease a baking sheet and lay out the bacon rashers in a line, not touching or overlapping.

Drizzle each rasher lightly with a little maple syrup.

Place in a moderately hot oven for appx 45 mins.

If you like the bacon to be a bit charred leave in for a bit longer.

Once cooked place on some paper towel and leave to cool.

Scotch Eggs

Chunky crumb coating, runny in the middle with a hint of sage and onion – perfect!

Ingredients (makes 4)

- 4 free range eggs
- 200g good quality sausage meat
- 1 small onion (minced)
- 2-3 pieces of stale bread (grated with a mix of fine and coarse)
- 1 beaten egg
- Good pinch of sage
- Oil for deep frying

Method

This bit can be a bit tricky if you want a runny middle as cooking times have to be exact and cooling immediately after.

For smallish sized eggs, that have been stored at room temperature, place in a pan of cold water and put on a high heat to boil.

As soon as it starts to boil, set the timer for 3 mins.

As soon as the time is up, remove from heat and run under cold water to stop them cooking further in the shells.

Peel the eggs and set to one side.

Knead the minced onion into the sausage meat and divide into 4 equal balls. Mould the sausage meat around each egg.

In a large bowl add breadcrumbs and sage, and roughly mix.

Take each Scotch egg, roll in the beaten egg, then in breadcrumbs and leave to one side, repeat the process until all have been coated.

Set the deep fat fryer to a moderate/high heat and cook one at a time until the outer crumb is golden and crunchy.

Great served on their own or on a bed of salad.

Roasted Apple & Smoked Bacon Wraps

Ingredients

- Smoked back bacon (allow 4 – 6 pieces person)
- Eating apples (thick quarters, allow one apple per 4/6 pieces of bacon)
- Apple sauce (1 tsp per rasher of bacon)
- Brown sugar (2-3 tsp)
- Rosemary or thyme sprigs (optional)

Method

Lightly grease a griddle pan.

Put a dollop of apple sauce on each rasher of bacon and roll up.

Place each rasher on the pan with a piece of apple on the top and sprinkle lightly with brown sugar.

Bake on a mod-high heat for 30 - 45 mins (depending on the thickness of your bacon)

Make sure you scrape up the caramelised bits on the bottom of the pan when serving, cos it's 'gert lush'.

Chicken

Roasted Garlic, Herb & Lemon Chicken

Ingredients

- Whole chicken
- 4 cloves garlic (minced)
- Half a tsp mixed herbs
- 1 lemon (quartered)
- 1 tbsp butter or oil
- Salt & pepper

Method

Place the chicken in a roasting pan.

Gently lift the skin on chicken so it comes away from the flesh by inserting your fingers underneath the skin and carefully working your way down the length of the bird.

Mix the garlic and herbs together and insert under the skin.

Place the lemon quarters inside the cavity.

Spread the butter over the skin and legs and season with salt & pepper.

Cook on a moderate to high heat.

To work out your cooking times, you should be allowing 20 mins per lb plus an extra 20 mins if you have used a stuffing, so it's worth keeping a note on the weight of the bird.

When the juices run clear and it falls away from the bone easily, it's usually a good indicator of readiness.

Chinese Orange Chicken

Ingredients for the chicken

- 4 chicken breasts or thighs (diced)
- 100g cornflour
- 100g plain flour
- 1 tsp baking powder
- ½ a teaspoon turmeric (for colour)
- Salt & pepper
- 1 small bottle of pale ale (lager will also suffice)
- 1-2 litres of sunflower oil, for frying

For the Sauce

- 2 cups orange juice
- 2 tbsp sugar
- 2 tbsp orange marmalade
- 4 tbsp rice vinegar
- 4 tbsp soy sauce
- 4 garlic cloves (crushed)
- ½ tsp ginger
- 2 chillies (sliced)
- 2 tbsp cornflour

Method for the chicken

Make the batter first to coat the chicken. Combine flours, beer, turmeric, baking powder, salt and pepper.

Put the oil on to heat.

Sprinkle some plain flour onto a plate, lightly toss each piece of chicken in it before coating it in the batter mix.

Doing small batches at a time, place in the hot oil and cook until golden.

Repeat until all the chicken is used up.

Place the chicken pieces to one side.

Optional garnish

- Orange slices
- Chopped spring onion
- Green chillies

Method for the sauce

Place all the ingredients (except cornflour) into a saucepan and heat gently.

Simmer for a few mins.

Mix the cornflour with a little water and gradually add to the orange sauce until the desired thickness is achieved.

Add the battered chicken to the sauce and stir.

Serve with noodles or rice and some stir fry veg.

Hot Smoked Chicken

Hot smoked chicken is fabulous served with anything! If you have never tried hot smoking before, it's well worth a try. You may find you need a few practice runs to master it, depending on your smoker. Things worth bearing in mind when smoking are the variables that can affect temperature control. Always use a good quality charcoal/chips. If the temperature outside is cold you will struggle to get the smoker up to temperature and keep it there so it's best attempted when the weather is warmer if you're a first timer. If you are confident enough, you can always smoke the chicken for an hour or so and finish off in the oven if the smoker can't maintain temperature in cooler months. There are many smokers on the market; my advice is to buy a cheap one to start with and see how you get on with it. If you decide you like hot smoking you can always upgrade at a later date to one which is better insulated, which means you don't have to work so hard at maintaining the temperature.

Ingredients

- Whole chicken
- Charcoal/chips
- Water (hot)
- Smoker

Method

Place charcoal/chips in the correct tray in the smoker and light.

Once it has caught sufficiently place the water tray over the top and add the hot water to it.

Place the griddle and lid on the top of the smoker and wait until the correct temperature is displayed on the heat thermometer.

Once an adequate heat has been reached, place the chicken inside and let the smoker do its thing!

Cook until juices run clear and use a temperature probe to ensure the chicken has reached a safe temperature.

Spit Roasted Chicken

Great in the summer to use over your BBQ and uses the same concept as a whole hog roast: slow cooked and lightly smoked at the same time.

Rotating spits for this purpose are easily obtained from the internet if you don't have an outdoor/camping shop near to you that sells them. So easy and so tasty!

Ingredients

- 1 whole chicken
- Seasoning
- Oil
- Chilli or BBQ sauce for basting towards the end (optional)
- Breads and salads to serve

Method

Light the BBQ. When the coals are glowing white, arrange them in the centre of the BBQ so they are situated directly below where the chicken will be rotating.

With coals glowing white and the chicken secured on the spit, lightly brush the bird in oil and season with salt and pepper.

Place the bird in situ and set the motor going.

If you want to get a sticky caramelised finish on the skin occasionally baste with a sweet chilli or BBQ sauce whilst it's cooking.

Grab a beer and kick your heels up whilst the bird cooks.

Make yourself comfy as you will have to tend the fire. Ideally you don't want bursts of flame but rather the embers as it's a consistent heat.

Don't forget the variables - outside temp, wind, etc - will have an effect on readiness; it could take a few hours.

If in doubt use a temperature probe.

Beef

Salted Beef

Ingredients

- 2kg lump of beef (brisket is a good cut for this)
- 900g salt
- 5 litres of hot water
- 3 tbsp black peppercorns
- 1 tbsp allspice

Method

Heave all the salt in a large plastic container (with lid) add the hot water, stir and add spices and peppercorns.

Allow to cool.

Add the lump of beef to the container and place the lid on.

Leave in the fridge for a week.

When the brining process is complete, remove meat and wash in clean water.

Place in a large saucepan of water and bring to the boil.

Reduce heat and simmer gently for 3 hours.

Great served hot with a creamy mash with added horseradish and seasonal veg or served cold with pickles, crusty breads, or crackers.

Chinese Braised Beef (slow cooker method)

A great dish you can bung in the slow cooker and forget for several hours. You can freeze any leftovers in individual portion sizes for a quick ready meal another day.

Ingredients

(serves 8-10)

- 2kg diced beef
- 3 large onions (peeled and roughly chopped)
- 1 bulb garlic (peeled)
- 1 large bunch coriander
- 3 tbsp Chinese 5-spice
- 4 inches root ginger (peeled)
- 150g brown sugar
- 200ml dark soy sauce
- 1.5 litres beef stock
- Oil for frying

Method

Place onions, garlic, ginger, and coriander in food processor and whiz up, then bung it in the slow cooker.

Add the sugar, 5-spice, soy sauce and stock, and combine.

Set the cooker to low whilst you brown the meat in a frying pan. You may have to brown it off in several batches. Once each batch is done, heave it in the slow cooker. Cook on low for 4 - 5 hours stirring occasionally.

Serve over a bed of rice or noodles with some stir fry Chinese leaf, carrot batons, water chestnuts and mushrooms, making sure you spoon plenty of that rich dark sauce over the top.

Hot Smoked Beef with Orange Marmalade Crust

As with the salted beef it's best to brine the beef for 2 or 3 days first.

Ingredients

- 2kg lump of beef (I used sirloin for this one but brisket will work as well)
- 3 litres water
- ½ cup salt
- ½ cup brown sugar
- ½ cup caster sugar
- 2 tbsp black peppercorns
- Orange marmalade

Method

In a large saucepan, place half the water and bring to the boil.

Add sugars, salt, and spices.

Stir until the sugar and salt are dissolved.

Remove from heat and add the rest of the water.

Place meat in a large enough container to allow the meat to be completely covered with the brine.

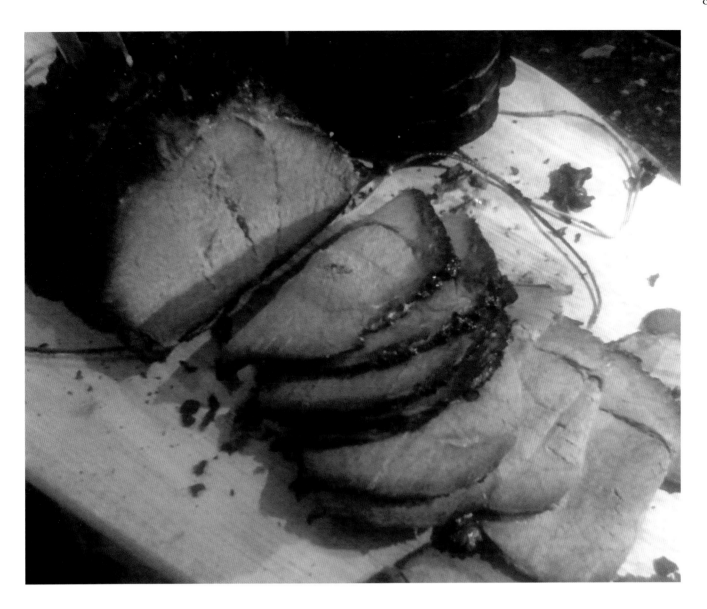

Once the brine is cold enough, pour over the meat, cover and place in the fridge for 2 - 3 days.

When the time is up, remove beef from the brine, rinse in fresh cold water and pat dry.

Spread a good thick coating of marmalade on the rind of the beef.

Brown the beef off under a grill, briefly (until a charred crust has formed from the marmalade).

Place the joint in a smoker.

The idea now is to cook the meat slowly in the smoker.

With the smoker lit and ready to go, place the meat on the wire rack in the smoker.

If you want to add smoking chips, do so now.

To avoid direct heat on the meat and the loss of moisture, use the water pan in the smoker filled with hot water to act as a buffer between the fire and meat.

Depending on the size of your joint and variables in the weather and charcoal quality cook on a low heat for several hours.

Beef Torrington

Mrs Slocombe's take on a beef Wellington: the 'Beef Torrington'.

I couldn't help but create this one around the strong cavalier theme that runs through this lovely little town.

I have in the past used steaks instead of a whole fillet of beef which is great if you like your beef 'proper' cooked and not still 'mooing' in the middle.

Don't be afraid to experiment with the outer layer on this one also. Minced mushroom and onion mixed with a pork pâté works well but equally a simple sage & onion stuffing coating is also very complimentary to the beef.

Ingredients

- Good quality fillet of beef (or steaks)
- Puff pastry (enough to cover the size of the fillet you are cooking).
- 1 cup minced mushrooms
- 1 small onion (finely diced)
- 1 tub pork pâté
- Bacon rashers or Parma ham (enough to cover the outside of the beef.
- 1 beaten egg yolk
- Oil for frying
- Slosh of white wine
- Fresh herbs for dressing

Method

If you need to shape the beef first, mould it to shape, wrap tightly in cling film and refrigerate overnight.

Lightly sear the outside of the beef in an oiled pan until cooked to your requirements. Allow to cool, wrap in film and refrigerate for appx 20 mins.

Next, make the duxelles.

Squeeze out any excess water from the mushrooms and place in an oiled frying pan with the onions. Add a splosh of wine and fry over a moderate heat until reduced. Add to the pâté and stir well.

Lay out a piece of cling film and lay the bacon out in strips, coat the bacon with duxelles and place the beef on top. Roll the film around the beef so it is encased.

Refrigerate again whilst you work on the pastry.

Dust the work surface with flour and roll out the pastry to desired size.

Remove the beef from the cling film and place on the pastry.

Cut pastry to size and glaze the edges of the pastry with the egg.

Wrap and seal edges.

Brush egg all over the pastry, season with rock salt ground pepper.

Bake in a preheated oven for appx 25 – 40 mins depending on the size.

Beef Torrington is my own fun take on the classic beef Wellington, featuring a special 'cavalier hat' pastry in honour of the Great Torrington Cavaliers.

The Great Torrington Cavaliers is a voluntary organisation that raises money for charity and good causes through high-profile public events.

They have been in existence since 1970 and have received international recognition for their giant themed bonfires, and firework displays.

At time of writing and publishing, they are building a full-size replica of the Mayflower for a huge bonfire celebration in 2020.

www.torrington-cavaliers.co.uk

Winners of the Queen's Award for Voluntary Service in 2016.

Sous Vide Beef Joints

You will need a sous vide bath for this, or a sous vide wand which you clip to the side of an ordinary pan, and suitable vacuum and seal bags.

Sous vide is a cooking technique which enables cooking at low temperatures for longer periods, losing very little fat and retaining full flavour. This technique is great if you are using a high-quality meat, such as I have here, and want to retain those essential omega 3 fats. The beef I used was my own, a UK native breed having lived on pasture only.

There are many ways to flavour your meat whilst in the bag; it's all down to your personal choice.

In this example I've used one joint with added orange wedges and the other I left plain, just a light seasoning of salt & pepper as the idea was to put a coarse grain mustard on one and orange marmalade on the other at the end of the sous vide process and finish it off under the grill until it was charred. Again it's all down to personal preference.

The sous vide method is also great for steaks (amongst a heap of other foods); simply cook in the bath for the desired finish - rare to well done - and then place on a griddle at high heat to get the seared finish.

Ingredients

- Good quality beef joints
- Orange wedges
- Salt & pepper
- Coarse grain mustard
- Orange marmalade

Method

Cut joints to desired size, place in bags, add orange wedges to one and lightly season the other with salt & pepper.

Vacuum seal the bags and place in the water bath.

Using the guidelines on your machine's instructions to get the desired finish for your meat, set your temperatures and cooking times accordingly.

At the end of the cooking time, preheat your grill to med-high heat, remove joints from bag (discard orange wedges) and place on a suitable roasting pan, spread the marmalade on one and mustard on the other.

Grill for 5 mins or until the coating has crusted the way you want it.

Lamb

Spit Roasted Lamb

You will need the following

- Hog roaster
- 3-4 10kg bags of lump wood charcoal
- Rosemary (optional)
- Lard
- 1 lamb (you can usually get these delivered to your site/venue straight from the butchers)
- Common sense and a sense of humour!

I love cooking over fire, a great focal point for a feast with a gathering. A whole lamb will easily feed 40 people so, if you are planning a big do, it may be worth considering hiring in a hog roaster for the day (if you don't own one). Here we cooked a lamb for a load of Vikings in the middle of a field on Exmoor in November, 'cos Mrs Slocombe really likes to make life difficult for herself! If you decide to do a whole pig instead of a lamb, in principle it's the same except you will need to rub lots of salt into the skin and it will take longer to cook than a lamb; typically, under normal conditions, 8 hours cooking time for a 65kg pig and this will easily serve 100.

Method

Get the fire in the roaster going so it will be ready for when you have prepped the lamb.

You will need to think about the position of the coals in relation to the dense points of the lamb to enable heat where it is needed the most.

So, you will want more heat at the foot and head end of 'Lamby' as that is where it is thickest and tapering away in the middle section where the chest cavity will be open and therefore not taking so long to cook.

To gauge the heat and position make sure it's close enough to cook but not so close it will burn.

You will need half an hour or so to get the lamb rigged up to the spit and secured on safely.

Once the lamb is safely on the spit rub some lard over the entire lamb.

Essential 'just in case' extras

- Fire extinguisher
- First aid box

To serve

- Fresh flour topped baps
- Mint yogurt
  or mint jelly

Method cont.

Providing there are no big flames from the roaster leaping up at you, you are now ready to place 'Lamby' in situ.

Rig up the spit to the motor and start it rotating.

Add a bit of common sense: if 'Lamby' starts burning raise the bar, if it doesn't look like it's cooking at all, lower the bar a tad.

You might find you are up and down every five mins raising and lowering, depending on wind direction and outside temperature.

If so, add some of your sense of humour to get you through!

Cooking times vary considerably and you will need to factor in things like the outside temperature (it takes considerably longer to cook in the winter than in summer months), the quality of the charcoal, size of the lamb and the experience of those cooking it.

Just ensure the juices run clear and it's hot at the thickest point before serving.

Lamb & Mint Skewers (serves 4)

Ingredients

- 500g lamb mince
- 1 large bunch fresh mint leaves (finely chopped)
- 1 red onion (finely minced in a processor)
- 2 tbsp sage & onion stuffing
- Salt & pepper
- Skewers

To serve

- 150ml pot plain yogurt
- Lambs lettuce, spinach leaves and rocket
- Naan breads

Method

Preheat the oven to a moderately high heat.

Remove one or two tsp of the fresh mint and stir into the yogurt.

In a large bowl bung in the lamb mince, mint, onion, and sage & onion stuffing. Season with salt & pepper and combine all the ingredients together.

Separate the mix into equal sized patties and roll between your hands to make a sausage shape, thread onto a skewer.

Repeat the process until all the mix is used.

Place the skewers on a non-stick baking sheet and bake for 20 - 30 mins.

5 mins before the lamb skewers are ready, sprinkle a little water on the naan breads and place in the oven.

Serve warm with the mint yogurt dip and salad.

Lemon & Mint Lamb Rack

Mint has always been a traditional accompaniment to lamb, of course, but the zing of lemon adds an extra dimension.

The smell in your kitchen when you cook this is heavenly!

The end result is a tender, moist meat with a charred outer, infused with a mild minty, citrus flavour.

Ingredients

- 1 rack of lamb
- 3 tbs walnut oil
- Juice of 1 lemon
- 1 - 2 tsp grated lemon zest
- ½ tsp cumin
- ½ tsp oregano
- 2 tbsp chopped mint leaves
- 1-2 cloves of garlic

Method

Place lamb on tin foil (leaving enough to wrap and cover the lamb entirely) and put in an ovenproof dish.

Place the rest of the ingredients in a pestle and mortar and give it a good squishing ensuring garlic cloves are squashed down.

Pour the mix over the lamb and fold the tin foil round it loosely.

Leave to marinade for min 2 hours - overnight.

When ready to cook, preheat the oven to a low/moderate heat and slow cook the lamb for 1½ - 2 hours.

When cooked, unwrap the foil and crank the heat up to get a charred finish on the skin.

I left mine for appx 30 mins at this stage as I personally love the charred taste and texture of the marinade on the skin also.

If you don't like it done quite so well you can of course remove it sooner, when it's done how you like it.

Nut Crusted Rack of Lamb with Herb Relish

Ingredients (serves 2)

- 2 x racks of lamb with 3 or 4 bones in each
- 1 tbsp almonds
- 1 tbsp mixed nuts (chopped)
- 1 tsp Dijon mustard
- 2 tbsp breadcrumbs
- 1 good handful of parsley (finely chopped)
- A little oil to bind

Method

Preheat oven to moderate heat.

Mix mustard, bread crumbs, parsley and nuts together and set to one side.

Score the lamb and place on a preheated lightly oiled griddle and sear the lamb all around.

Wrap the lamb in tin foil and place in the oven for appx 40 mins.

Remove from the oven, open foil and place the crust mix on top of the lamb, fat side up.

Place back in the oven for appx 30 mins, with the foil open.

If you like quite a browned top you can always place under the grill at the end of cooking time to brown off.

Relish

- 1 large bunch fresh mint (I also added a tsp of dried mint as I like the texture)
- 1 small bunch fresh parsley
- 1 tbsp sugar
- 50ml malt vinegar
- 1 tbsp rapeseed oil

For the Relish

Put the sugar on the chopping board and chop the herbs into the sugar ensuring you scrape and mix it in well.

Place vinegar in a small saucepan and bring to a simmer.

Add herbs and sugar and simmer for 3 mins.

Allow to cool and add the oil to the mix to give a little texture.

Road-Kill!

The following recipe is somewhat serendipitous as the incident occurred while writing the book. Although it's a horrid thing to happen, there really is no point in wasting it. In this case the specific road-kill was a pheasant.

It is widely accepted that it is illegal to use road-kill for yourself if it was your car that killed it. After some research it appears this is somewhat a grey area, with the relevant section of law being section 11 of the Wildlife and Countryside Act 1981. However, this book is not intended as a legal reference work and you should not produce it in a court of law if ever prosecuted under said act.

A big problem with road-kill is that it may have been run over several times by other vehicles or pecked at by carrion birds such as crows. Also, let's not forget that any animal lying dead by the roadside might have been poisoned or died from disease. Therefore, unless you are very brave or desperate, it is best to avoid those unfortunate creatures which are already long dead.

This particular pheasant, however, leapt out of the hedge and straight under the vehicle in front. There was no time for the driver to react, indeed they may even have been blissfully unaware, and the bird was therefore, literally, fair game for me.

Taking care to avoid danger to yourself and other road users, make sure it is actually dead and not suffering, if it is still alive but badly injured, you have to decide if it requires a trip to the nearest vet or the coup de grâce. If the latter, you also need to consider how the law stands regarding further culinary activity. I cannot give you adequate legal advice here, other than the bare minimum of don't get caught!

Anyway, when you have retrieved your bird from the road, you will then need to let it hang for a few days. A cool garage or cellar will do.

Pluck it and cut off the best bits. Avoid cutting the crop area, (situated just above the breast) as this will be full of the pheasant's last meal.

When you have done this, give it a good wash. It is then ready to use.

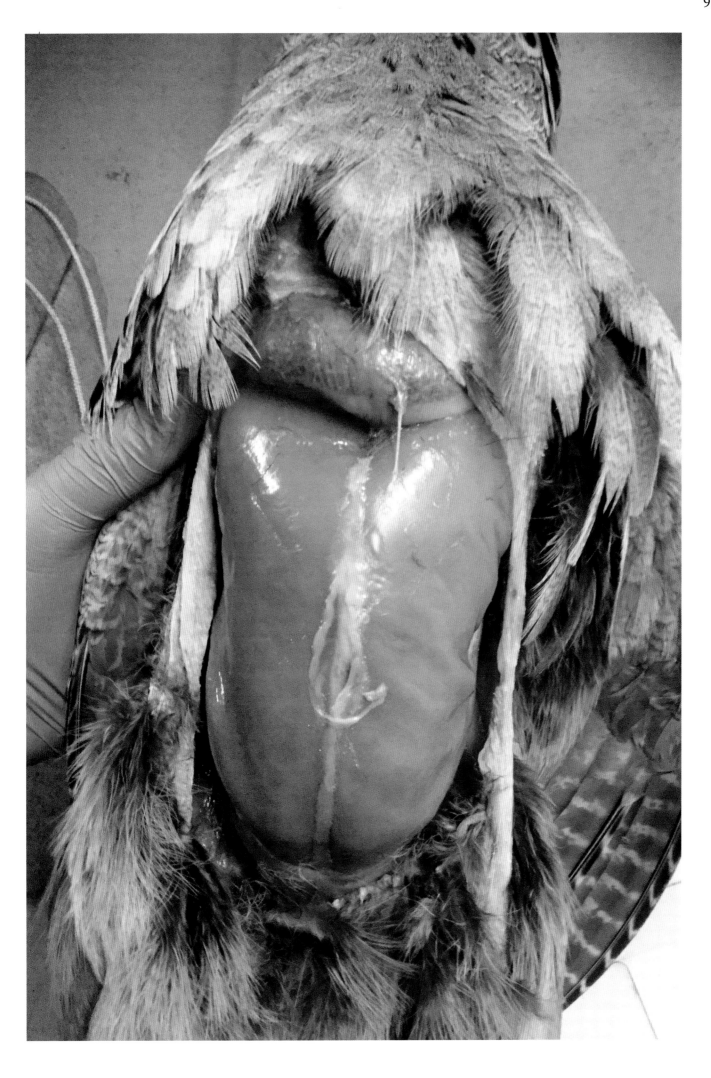

Pheasant, Bacon, Chestnut and Cherry Pie

Ingredients

- Pheasant (diced)
- 6 bacon rashers (cut into short strips)
- 1 red onion (diced)
- 2 cloves garlic (crushed)
- 1 pint chicken stock
- 1 jar Morello cherries

Method

Place meat, stock, wine, brandy, juice from the cherries, and the herbs in a slow cooker, set to low heat and cook for 4 hours.

Line a fairly deep pie dish or cake tin with baking parchment.

Use the base of the tin as a guide to cut the pastry, allow an overlap of appx 2 inches.

Place the pastry in the tin, place another piece of baking parchment on the top and fill with baking beans.

Work your way around the tin folding and pinching the edges of the pastry.

- 1 cup cooked chestnuts (peeled)
- Good slosh red wine
- A splash of brandy
- Pinch of nutmeg
- Pinch of thyme
- Pinch of rosemary
- Shortcrust pastry (see my shortcrust pastry recipe)
- Cornflour to thicken stock

30 mins before the cook time is up on the slow cooker, preheat the oven to a med/high setting and put the pastry in for 20 mins.

Use the cornflour to thicken the stock in the slow cooker.

When the pastry is cooked, carefully remove the baking beans and the baking parchment they are on.

Add the contents from the slow cooker to the pastry, top with the chestnuts and cherries and return to the oven for 10 - 15 mins.

Mrs Slocombe goes Fishing

Fish on a Stick

This is a great snack for surfers, inspired by Mrs Slocombe's son, Zak.

Not too heavy, minimal faffing around and no fancy equipment needed.

P.S. Don't add the beer unless you've finished surfing for the day and, of course, only if someone else is driving you home.

Ingredients

- However many fish you think you can eat
- A rock
- A fire
- Sufficient sticks or skewers for the number of fish
- Beer (optional)

Method

Catch fish. (Alternatively, buy from fishmonger and pretend you caught it.)

Assuming it's not a shark, hit head with priest or similar heavy, blunt object to ensure a humane despatch (that's the fish's head not yours!).

Make a slit on belly and remove guts (again, we're referring to fish's guts, not your own).

Find clean thin stick, assuming you haven't thought ahead and brought a skewer.

Insert stick/skewer up rectum (as aforementioned; not your own!).

(Publisher's note, fish do not technically have a rectum, but this is a cookery book not GCSE biology.)

Slap the fish on the BBQ (lit).

Cook until browned and sizzling well.

Serve with an ice-cold beer and chomp straight off the stick!

Soused Mackerel

Ingredients (serves 2)

- 2 whole mackerel
- 100ml malt vinegar
- 75ml white wine vinegar
- 30g caster sugar
- 1 red chilli (finely chopped)
- 2 bay leaves
- 1 tbsp black peppercorns
- 2 wedges of lemon

Method

Preheat the oven to 200°C fan/ 220°C/gas 7.

Place the mackerel in an ovenproof dish.

Put the remaining ingredients (apart from the lemon) in a saucepan and bring to the boil, simmer for a few minutes.

Pour the liquid over the mackerel and cover with foil.

Bake for 20 mins.

Serve with warm crusty bread and a squeeze of lemon juice.

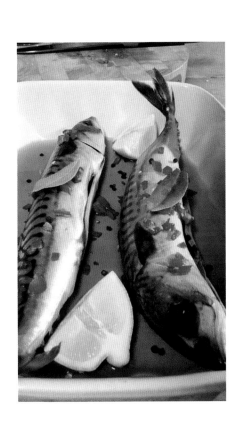

Cheese Crusted Smoked Basa

Ingredients (Serves 2)

- 2 fillets of smoked basa
- 50g breadcrumbs
- 20g grated parmesan cheese
- 150g soft cheese
- Black pepper
- Fresh parsley to garnish (chopped)

Method

Season the fish with pepper.

Melt the butter in a frying pan and add the fish.

Fry on each side for a few minutes.

Remove pan from heat.

Preheat the grill on a mod-high heat.

Leave the fish in the pan and spread the soft cheese evenly between the 2 fillets.

Sprinkle the breadcrumbs on top of the soft cheese, followed by the parmesan.

Place the frying pan under the grill to brown the top of the crumbs.

Serving suggestion

This dish goes well with baby potatoes, sugar snap peas, baby corn and fine green beans and also lends itself as well with a light salad and fresh crusty bread. Any butter left over in the pan, use to drizzle over the new potatoes.

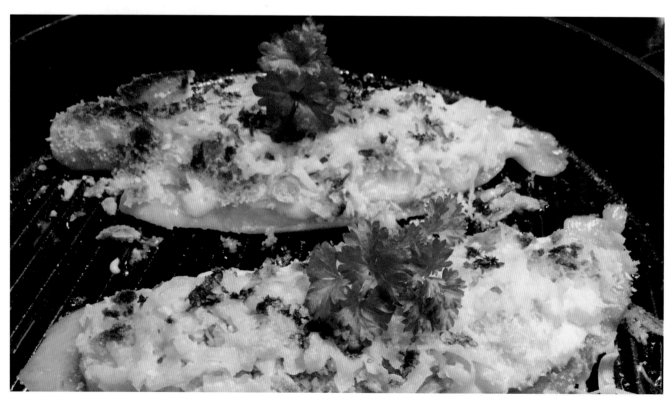

Poppy & Sesame Crusted Tuna Steaks

Ingredients (serves 2)

- 2 Tuna steaks
- Egg white
- 2 tbsp poppy seeds
- 2 tbsp sesame seeds
- Rapeseed oil for frying

Method

Crack an egg white out onto a plate.

On another plate combine the seeds.

Toss the tuna steaks in the egg white to ensure an even coating on both sides and along the edges, then flop it around in the seeds until completely covered.

On a medium heat, heat the oil, add the tuna steaks and turn frequently.

Getting it just right

Fish doesn't take long to cook, if you want a finish like a rare steak where it retains the pinkness in the middle then it will take appx 3 - 4 mins depending on the thickness of the steaks.

If, like me, you want it totally cooked (where all the flesh is white and it's not looking like it's going to start flapping around on the plate) let it cook for appx 6 - 8 mins.

Tip

This dish is fab served with noodles, nuts and stir fry veg, with added rice vinegar, chilli sauce and soy sauce added to the wok.

Sticky Glazed Haddock

Ingredients (serves 4)

- 4 haddock fillets (skinless)
- 2 tablespoons clear runny honey
- 2 tablespoons rice vinegar
- 1 tablespoon soy sauce
- 2 garlic cloves (minced)
- 1 inch ginger (grated)
- 6 tbsp passata or puréed tomatoes
- 2 teaspoons sesame oil
- 2 red chillies (finely chopped)
- 4 teaspoons sesame seeds (for decorating)

Note,

If you have had a go at making my "Ring Ripper" sweet chilli relish (see page 45) and you still have some left, you could always heave a bit of soy sauce in it. The result is near enough the same and a good plan 'B' if you don't have all the ingredients above handy.

Method

Line a baking sheet/ roasting tray with foil and brush with oil.

Place the haddock on the foil.

Combine the rest of the ingredients together in a bowl, apart from the sesame seeds and oil.

Brush the mix onto the fish, encase in the foil and refrigerate for 24 hours to get the maximum flavour infusion.

If you haven't got 24 hours, a few hours will suffice but longer is preferred.

Preheat the oven to a moderately hot heat.

Remove the top layer of foil and place under a hot grill until the glaze is slightly charred and sizzling.

Remove from the grill, brush some more sesame oil around the fish and under the fish and, using the remaining glaze, cover the fish.

Bake in the oven for a further 10 mins.

During the last five mins of cooking time, place sesame seeds on a suitable tray and place in the oven to lightly toast.

Sprinkle on the fish when serving.

Fish doesn't take long to cook generally but if your fillets are on the thicker side, cooking times may need to be adjusted.

Please ensure it's piping hot throughout and flakes away easily.

This dish is great with steamed veg and rice.

Tip

If you have a spare red or green pepper, cut in half, wash, de-seed,

Brush with a little oil and roast in the oven for 5-10 mins and use it to serve the rice in.

Salmon Gateau

This is absolutely fabulous as a sharing platter, served with some crackers on the side to give more texture.

Ingredients (serves 6)

- 400g smoked salmon (chopped, but keep some back uncut to make a rose out of for the top)
- 50g soft cheese
- 6 Carrots (grated)
- Pine nuts (lightly toasted)
- 4 cups of grated potato (cooked)
- 1 red onion (finely diced)
- Cucumber (to decorate)
- 4 small cooked beetroot (shredded)
- 300g mayonnaise
- 1 round white or wholemeal loaf (crusts removed)
- Fresh herbs; basil, parsley
- Watercress and wild rocket to decorate
- Black pepper

Method

Remove the bottom of a loose based cake tin and place the wall of it on the plate/cake stand you intend to serve the gateau on.

Microwave the shredded potato for appx 10 mins, drain in a colander and pour a kettle full of freshly boiled water over to remove some of the starch.

Set to one side to cool then add some mayo, pepper, red onion and stir.

Grate carrots, add the pine nuts and a little mayonnaise, stir to combine.

Slice a piece of bread off (across) and use the base of the cake tin to cut round the bread to get the right size.

Spread some cream cheese on the bread and place inside the cake tin to form the bottom layer.

Mix the chopped salmon together using appx one tbsp of the mayo: just enough to help bind it together but not mar the vibrant colour of the salmon.

Spread this on top of the previous layer and even out firmly.

Spread half of the potato and onion mix on top of the salmon.

Spread the carrot mix on next.

Spread remaining potato mix on top of carrot.

Mix ¾ of the beetroot with mayo (appx 1 tbsp), spread on the last layer.

Sprinkle the remaining beetroot over the top.

Make your rose out of the remaining salmon by rolling and manipulating into the shape of a rose.

Method cont.

Use some salad leaves to arrange around the rose to appear like petals.

Place on the gateau.

Chill for several hours.

When ready to serve, carefully remove the wall of the cake tin.

Decorate with sprigs of fresh herbs and any remaining salad leaves as desired.

Tip

For easier cutting, remove the salad leaves from the top and place the salmon gateau in the freezer for 30 mins.

Grandma's Kitchen

My fantabulous Nanny Hoot, I used to love my visits to see you, always heading straight for your pantry, knowing full well you would have made something for me. Thank you for giving me some wonderful childhood memories, for teaching me never to eat cheese straight from the fridge but to let it come up to room temperature first, else it would be 'yukums' as you used to say. Thank you for introducing me to and connecting me with the real food ethos; homemade food from scratch, with fruits, herbs and vegetables straight from your garden, or the local farm. Thanks for the eggs which you sent me to fetch for you, and for taking me to your favourite butcher and fishmonger. You always sourced the best. Your teaching stuck with me whilst growing up and still does today.

I never used to mind fetching you vegetables from your garden as it was an excuse to go and talk to the cows in the field at the far end but I did get told off for climbing over the fence to get in there with them.

I remember, as well, the time you sent me out to the garden to get something for you and I froze at the sight of a big black adder in my path, screaming my head off. Out you trotted, this doughty little old bird, armed with a huge concrete block calmly standing over it, dumping it on his head and saying, "There you go, you can carry on now," and off you went back indoors to finish making your pastry!

I can honestly say I can't remember you ever having a cooking disaster and nor can anyone else apart from one time a label fell off your homemade apple pie in the freezer and you thought it was steak and kidney. Dishing it up with veg, mash and gravy for my Uncle Peter and his girlfriend, whom he'd brought round for tea for the first time, must have been one of the most awkward meals you'd ever had!

Thanks for the wonderful breads, biscuits, tarts and cakes too. I remember rock cakes, 'rockers' as you used to call them, the size of side plates! I make these following your recipe to the dot and enjoy the nostalgia trip as much as I do eating them and sharing them around, just as you did!

Freda Gertrude Cole

23/1/1923 - 7/2/2014

Creative Victoria Sponges

It's great to get a bit creative with cakes and buttercream.

These looks can be achieved with piping nozzles, a bit of practice and getting the wrist action just right at the right time.

For best results with the piping nozzles the buttercream needs to be of a fairly stiff consistency, if it's too soft the flowers will collapse.

As you squeeze and draw the piping bag up you need to twist the wrist at the point of finishing to release the flower.

Have a practice on a plate for a while before attempting to get them on the cake.

If you fancy getting more creative and to achieve the effect of two-tone flowers, before you fill the piping bag with buttercream, take a cocktail stick, dip in food colouring gel and draw random streaks of colour on the inside of the bag.

Another way to achieve this is to take a piece of cling film laid out flat and draw streaks on the film.

Place the butter icing on it in a sausage-like shape.

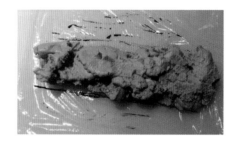

Roll up the film, twist the ends off.

Then cut one end and drop the whole thing in an icing bag.

Another good tip is when covering an entire cake with a buttercream is to keep dipping your palette knife in hot water, shake off excess and apply immediately to the buttercream; it's much easier to work with.

Ingredients (sponge cake)

- 200g baking spread or unsalted butter
- 200g caster sugar
- 200g self-raising flour
- 4 eggs
- 1 teaspoon baking powder
- Buttercream (see method overleaf)

Sponge cake Method

Heave the whole lot in a mixing bowl and use a hand whisk to combine.

Stop mixing as soon as it's combined as over whisking can cause problems with a cake becoming heavy and dense.

Spread the batter evenly between 2 lined sandwich tins and bake in a preheated oven, 180°C fan/200°C/gas 4, for appx 20 mins.

Don't be tempted to open the oven door before it's reached the end of the cooking time as this will more than likely lead to it sinking.

Check the cake is cooked right through by inserting a thin skewer; it should come out clean, if not, return to the oven for a few more mins.

Turn out and allow to cool on a wire rack.

N.B.

If you decide to make a chocolate sponge add 50g cocoa powder the above, a small bag of choc chips and a splash of milk.

Buttercream method

Make life easy for yourself and start by softening the butter in the microwave for a few seconds.

Sift in the icing sugar ensuring it is lump free.

Stir until combined and add flavouring and colouring as required.

Tip

For the butter icing I always work on a principle of doubling the icing sugar weight to the butter weight, depending on the coverage you wish to achieve.

For example, 250g butter to 500g icing sugar will provide enough buttercream for a thick layer to the inside of a Victoria sandwich.

For colourings I prefer to use a food colour gel.

Rice Pudding (The Easy Way)

There was nothing better than a rice pudding cooked from the solid fuel Rayburn.

A firm favourite with Nan Snowy.

For those of you that have an electric or gas oven this process is straight forward...

The 'hard way' further down the page gives a valuable insight into life with a Rayburn.

Ingredients (serves 4)

- 2 pints full fat milk
- 140g pudding rice
- 110g caster sugar
- Knob of butter
- 1-2 teaspoons nutmeg

Method

Heat oven to 140°C fan/160°C/gas 3.

Use the knob of butter to grease an ovenproof dish.

In a saucepan, bring the milk to a simmer and add the rice and sugar, stirring all the time.

When the sugar has dissolved pour into the greased dish.

Sprinkle the top with nutmeg.

Bake for 1½ hours, stirring a couple of times through cooking.

Rice Pudding (The Traditional Way)

(or the hard way if you're not quite right in the head, you've taken leave of your senses and want to re-visit the good ole' days!)

This romantic ideology v the reality… Nan Snowy's rice pudding done in a solid fuel Rayburn. Made with unfiltered milk straight from the udder 'old stylie' (serves 4 unless you're a farmer then it serves 1).

Added ingredients to the above –

- A PhD in Rayburn psychology
- Patience
- A sense of humour
- Your best running wellies (you've got to catch the bad tempered Jersey yet!)
- Band Aid to the ready (not the 1980s super-group!)
- A wheel-barrow of wood; mix of dry, wet, big and small for optimum temperature control (ha-ha) expect anything from a tepid smoulder to a raging furnace!)

Also…

You will also need to check the speed and direction of the wind as this affects the burning rate as it howls down the chimney…

You might also need a 12-bore shotgun and a paper bag.

Now might also be a good time, for those that don't come from a farming background and weren't dragged up rough, tough and hard to bluff, to complete a risk assessment.

Rice puddings can be dangerous.

Cooking time

A 'when it's cooked' approach is needed here as it can be any time with all the variables considered, a rough guess of 3 – 9 hours will be bang on! New to Rayburns? Just do the best you can!

Method for cooking

Just heave all the ingredients in the oven proof dish. For good measure add extra butter and double cream to the Jersey cow's milk, sprinkle nutmeg on the top.

Take no notice of the oven temperature; it is what it is and it will do what it'll do! Just so long as it's a bit hotter than the room it's in, it'll be fine....eventually!

Bung it in the oven and shut the door as fast as you can. At this point you might feel you need to start talking nicely to your Rayburn in the hope it may just show you some compassion and behave itself (god you're funny!).

Please resist this urge to start talking to it. It's laughing at you, mocking you. As soon as you put that pud in, (he knows what he's about) the temperature sinks right back to cold! This is where you need the determination of a bull...

You-v-Rayburn! Game on!

You now need a copious amount of small dry sticks and wind! Open the top and bottom vents. Resume your position in front of the fire chamber door, psych yourself up with a handful of sticks ready in one hand, open the door to the fire chamber and let 'the awkward cantankerous beast' have it! Shut the door and wait...

If you have no wind from above to fan it, don't worry, you can get it in through the bottom vent. Wind might be available from various resources (use your imagination) start off by getting down on all fours, take a deep breath and blow for all you're worth into the bottom vent... you hear a 'whoosh' as it catches... great! Go in again!

At this point be careful not to get the carbon dioxide and oxygen levels out of sync (yours not the Rayburn). If you start to feel faint and it's not from being in a 'head down arse in air' position for too long, grab the paper bag and breathe into it until you start to feel better again.

After you've successfully made yourself hyperventilate, a sensible approach is needed: look to source wind elsewhere.

Plan 'B' is where the aged old dog with a flatulence problem suddenly becomes your best friend... The only problem is it can't let one rip to command!

Plan 'C' the hairdryer, plug in and point at the bottom vent...

Roaring, spitting crackling... Result!

You leave it go a few minutes before opening the door and chucking in some more dry wood hoping to retain this joyous moment of victory...

Don't be fooled... The oven gets so hot the needle goes round the dial, twice!

It wants you to open the oven door... Don't do it! It's a

trick! Instead, throw the biggest wettest log you can find in the chamber to calm it the hell down...

You can start to relax when you see the

oven dial begin to slip back to a moderate heat...Victory!

Don't be silly!

It's now got the hump, big time...

You realise this when you hear a bit too much crackling coming from the chimney...

Step outside just to check. If you have what resembles a rocket launcher preparing for take-off coming out from your roof, run back in and get the 12 bore!

Open all available windows and doors in the kitchen, with the fire in the chamber calmed down by the wet corner of rain forest you let it have earlier, you should be able to touch the pipe leading to the chimney safely with a cloth. Remove it and fire the shotgun up the chimney. Jobs a good un'! You now have control of the situation again.

By the time you've cleared up the mess, popped your dislocated shoulder back in, washed the soot off your mush and brushed your

hair, your pudding might be ready...

When it resembles a cooked appearance (if it hasn't been in there for days and walked off which, let's face it, if the scenario above has just happened it's unlikely) you're good to go!

Serve in a bowl/dish/bucket/whatever, with a shovel full of whatever flavoured jam you have available to hand at the bottom of your chosen serving vessel.

Don't forget a generous dollop of clotted cream on the top too...

For those of you that haven't made it this far, perhaps as a result of calling an ambulance 'cos you've had a coronary chasing the cow, or a nasty hoof to the head, or the kick from the 12 bore has rendered you unconscious, or you've had the biggest panic attack of your life, or perhaps because you've been arrested for air pollution and attempted arson; better luck next time you decide to use that romantic nice-looking smouldering demon

sat in the corner of your kitchen!

Well done to those that have made it this far; you're not quite out of the woods yet though...

This rich, calorie laden, cholesterol enhancing, sweet treat might just try and finish you off where the cow and Rayburn failed, so you might still need that ambulance!

Old skool farmers, put yer feet up and take a nap with your full contented belly!

South Molten

A mound of triple chocolate steamed pudding with an orange marmalade centre, named in honour of South Molton. Best served hot!

Ingredients

- 75g self-raising flour
- 25g cornflour
- 50g cocoa powder
- 100g unsalted butter or margarine
- 100g caster sugar
- 2 eggs
- Splash of milk
- 1 tsp baking powder
- ½ packet chocolate drops
- 1-2 tbsp orange marmalade
- 150g milk chocolate
- 1 orange (sliced)

Method

In a large mixing bowl, place flours, butter, cocoa, sugar, eggs, milk and baking powder and whisk until combined.

Stir in the chocolate drops.

Lightly grease and flour a pudding basin or large deep cereal bowl, add the mix to the bowl and cover with foil.

Place the bowl in a saucepan of boiling water. You want enough water in it to come approximately halfway up the bowl.

Allow the pudding to steam gently on a low heat for appx 1½ hours.

When the pudding is ready, start to melt the chocolate.

Turn the pudding out onto a serving plate and using a knife, cut a circular well in the top centre of the pudding and fill with orange marmalade.

Cover the pudding in the melted chocolate and serve immediately with freshly sliced orange.

Old Fashioned Rock Cakes

Nanny Hoot's rock cakes were the size of saucers! It's up to you of course how big you make these just adjust the cooking times accordingly.

Ingredients

- 340g self raising flour
- Pinch of salt
- 2 tsp nutmeg
- 1 tsp allspice
- 170g butter or margarine
- 170g caster sugar
- 170g mixed fruit
- 2 egg yolks
- Dash of milk to blend

Method

Place flour, butter, spices and salt into a bowl and mix.

Add the sugar and fruit and mix well.

Add egg yolks and milk and mix to form a stiff dough.

Separate the cake mix into desired sizes and arrange on a lined baking sheet.

Bake for 20 - 30 mins 180°C fan/200°C/gas 6.

Tea Leaf Reading

Ingredients

- For this, you will need a teapot, cups and saucers, and loose tea.

Method

Add 3 – 4 teaspoons of loose tea to a pre-warmed teapot.

Allow it to stew for a few mins and stir a couple of times before pouring.

Just before you pour, be sure to gently swizzle the teapot round to unsettle the tea leaves from the bottom of the pot; you want them to come out in the cup.

Pour tea into the teacup, add milk if desired and drink as you normally would. Have top ups too, again making sure you agitate the leaves at the bottom of the teapot each time you pour.

The tea leaves in your cup will settle to the bottom, please don't forget this!

A gob full of tea leaves will make you gag!

With just a little of the tea left in the cup, you only need enough to swish round and make the tea leaves stick to the sides of the cup.

Satisfied you have created a good display of scattered leaves stuck to the cup, immediately tip the cup upside down on the saucer and turn the cup round 3 times on the saucer and leave for a minute or so to drain.

They are now ready to be read!

Study the tea leaves hard, move the cup around and look for different angles.

The following symbols indicate their meanings.

The position they are in the cup indicate distance, e.g. if you see a journey symbol in the bottom of the cup it means a journey is expected in the future.

If it's positioned at the top of the cup it means the journey will happen very soon.

If the tea leaves are showing the present, they will be on the rim.

- A worm – indicates a journey.
- A spider – coming into some money.
- An owl – symbolises a warning of sickness, poverty and advises against starting out on a new project or venture.
- A heart (if positioned at or near the top) – symbolises good luck, joy, romance, and friendship.
- If it's at the bottom it could represent heartache or disappointment.
- An acorn – good health.
- Birds – lucky symbols. You will receive a letter or message.
- If a bird is at rest near a journey, the journey will be a good one.
- An elephant – good luck, health, and happiness.
- Triangle – good fortune is coming your way!

Shortbread

Ingredients

- 200g unsalted butter (softened)
- 60g caster sugar
- 300g plain flour
- 2 tsp vanilla extract

Method

Cream the butter and sugar together using a wooden spoon or a food processor and mix until it's fluffy.

Add vanilla essence and beat again.

Add the flours and mix until smooth.

With all the mixture combined, place into the bottom of a lined loose-bottomed cake tin and press down firmly creating an even surface.

Randomly prick with a fork and, using a thick knife, make 6 - 8 scores.

Alternatively, roll out, use pastry cutters to make into individual biscuits, and arrange on a baking sheet.

Leave to rest on side in a cool room or the fridge for 30 mins.

In a preheated oven of 150°C fan/170°C/ gas 3, bake for 30 – 40 mins until golden.

Remove from the oven and lightly sprinkle with caster sugar or icing sugar.

Allow to cool on a wire rack.

Serve with fresh strawberries or jam and a cup of tea!

Melt in the Mouth Shortcrust Pastry
Savoury

Use this pastry for any of your savoury pies. I always use a food processor to make mine as this keeps it as cold as possible and avoids over working it, I get perfect results every time using this method.

Ingredients

- 450g self-raising flour
- 3 or 4 tbsp of cornflour
- 225g good quality soft baking spread/margarine
- 1 egg
- Pinch of salt
- Ice cold water as needed

Tip

Replacing some of the self-raising flour with cornflour improves the pastry texture. Just remember, if you add a few tablespoons of cornflour, to remove an equal amount of self-raising flour.

Method

Place the margarine, salt and flour in the food processor and give it a brief whiz up until it's all combined. Add the egg and whiz up again until combined. Depending on the size of the egg used, I don't always have to add any water to completely combine. If you do add have to add water, make sure it's really cold and added to the processor whilst still in motion and just a tiny amount at a time.

Remove the pastry from the processor, wrap in cling film and bung it in the fridge for a couple of hours. When ready for use, roll out on a lightly floured surface, handling as little as possible.

Sweet Pastry

Same as above minus the salt, remove 2 tbsp of the self-raising flour and replace with icing sugar.

Beer Battered Cod Goujons

Nanny Hoot loved fish. Her beer battered cod, light and crispy, with homemade chips, was second to none; it was equally as good served with her own new potatoes dug fresh from the garden along with her fresh mint…

A tip for chopping the mint if you decide to use it: put half a teaspoon of sugar on the chopping board and finely chop the mint on top of the sugar to give it a little sweetness.

Ingredients

- 100g cornflour
- 100g plain flour
- 1 tsp baking powder
- ½ a teaspoon turmeric (for colour)
- Salt & pepper
- 1 small bottle of pale ale (lager will also suffice)
- 1-2 litres of sunflower oil, for frying
- 400g of filleted cod whole or cut into strips for goujons. (Hake or haddock also works well.)

Method

Combine flours, turmeric, baking powder in a bowl and season with a little salt & pepper.

Spoon enough of the dry mix out to toss the fish in before battering, appx 2 tbsp.

Add the beer a little at a time and stir until you are left with a thick, lump-free, batter mix.

Neck the rest of the beer!

Leave it to rest for 30 mins or so (the batter, not the remaining beer).

If you don't have a deep fat fryer, a large deep saucepan can be used.

Be careful and ensure you allow enough space for the fat to bubble up, and extra for when the fish is dropped in. Never fill a pan more than a third full of oil.

Put the oil on to heat.

Pat the fish dry with some paper towel.

Put the flour you set to one side on a plate and use to coat the fish; just toss each side briefly and shake off excess.

Place the fish in the batter mix.

Carefully drop the battered fish into the oil and fry for appx 6 - 8 mins.

Drain the fish on paper towel and season with sea salt.

Serve with homemade chips or minted new potatoes, mushy peas and tartare sauce.

Tip

Before dropping the fish in the fryer, make sure the oil is hot enough. To do this, drop a small amount of batter in the oil, if it bubbles up and crisps straight away, you're good to go!

Safety

NEVER leave the hot pan unattended. Oil can catch fire very easily. If this happens, do not move the pan. Instead, turn off heat only if it is safe to do so and allow the pan to cool completely. If you have a fire blanket, throw this over the flames if you can do so without risk to yourself but do not, under any circumstances, apply water to the fire. If in doubt, call the fire brigade.

Beef Hot Pot

Nanny Hoot really loved her vegetable garden and being as self-sufficient as possible; everything tasted better too.

I used to enjoy the errand of going to dig, pick, or pull the vegetables and fruits she needed for that day's meal.

Ingredients

- 1kg braising steak
- 1 tbsp sunflower oil
- 75g butter
- 2 medium onions (diced)
- 2 sticks celery (finely diced)

Method

Preheat the oven to 160°C fan/170°C/gas 3.

Heat the oil and half the butter in a large casserole pan.

Add the beef to the pan and season with salt and pepper.

Brown the meat all over.

In another large pan, add the remaining butter and heat.

Add onions and celery and lightly brown.

Add the carrots and cook for 2 mins.

Ingredients cont.

- 6 carrots (peeled and sliced into large chunks)
- 200ml red wine
- 400ml beef stock
- 1.5kg potatoes (sliced, ¼ inch thick)
- Salt & pepper
- Bouquet garni
- 1 tbsp plain flour

Method cont.

Add the flour and stir in.

Gradually add the beef stock and wine, stirring all the time until smooth.

Add this to the browned beef in the casserole pan.

Season again with salt and pepper and add the bouquet garni.

Bring to the boil. Remove from the boil and arrange the sliced potatoes on the top.

Season well with pepper and a touch of salt.

Cover the casserole pan with a lid and cook in the oven for appx 1 hour.

After one hour remove the lid, increase the heat by 30°C/ gas 3 and cook for a further 30 - 45 mins.

Milton Damerel Pork Pie

(Mrs Slocombe's take on Melton Mowbray)

For me, there is nothing better than a nice peppery pork pie loaded with gelatine! Unfortunately these little pieces of heaven seem to be increasingly hard to come by now a days, so, if you want anything doing right, do it yourself! This recipe uses a hot water crust pastry.

Ingredients

- 500g pork mince or chopped belly pork
- 300g smoked bacon (finely chopped)
- ½ teaspoon nutmeg
- ¼ tsp fresh sage (chopped)
- ¼ tsp fresh thyme (chopped)
- 1 tsp salt
- 2 tsp ground white pepper

Pastry

- 575g plain flour
- 200g lard or margarine
- 220ml water
- 1 beaten egg

Gelatin Filling

- 6 leaves of gelatin
- 300ml chicken stock

Method

Mix all the ingredients for the filling in a large bowl and set to one side.

For the pastry, line the base of a loose-bottomed 20cm standard cake tin or 10cm deep cake tin.

Heat the lard and water gently in a small pan until all the lard has melted.

Pour the mix onto the flour and stir well with a wooden spoon.

When the mix is cool enough to handle but still warm, knead well or until smooth. The pastry is easier to work with whilst warm as it will be pliable, so keeping it warm and working fast is the key to success.

Pull a chunk of the dough off, enough for the pastry lid, wrap in foil and set to one side.

Roll dough out in a circle twice as big as the cake tin base.

Place rolled dough in the base of the cake tin and gently work it up the sides of the pan.

Fill the tin with the pork mix and press down firmly.

Using a pastry brush, coat the visible pastry with the beaten egg.

With the remaining pastry roll out the lid, place on top of the pie and using your fingers pinch the top of the pie to the sides.

Now make a hole in the top of the pie using the back-end of a wooden spoon or similar. The idea of the hole is to pour in the gelatin later on and to let any steam out during cooking.

Preheat oven to 180°C/160°C fan/gas 4.

Place pie in the oven on a baking sheet (to catch any drips) and bake in the oven for the first 30 mins at the preheated temperature.

Then reduce down to 160°C/140°C fan/gas 3 and cook for a further 90 minutes.

When the remaining cooking time is down to the last 20 mins, remove the pie, brush the top with the remaining egg and return to the oven until cooked.

If you've opted for the deeper pie tin then add an extra 30 mins to cooking time.

Using a temperature probe the centre of the pie should reach

75°C so cook for a bit longer if required.

Soak the gelatin in cold water for 5 mins, remove and squeeze out excess water.

Bring the chicken stock to almost boiling point.

Remove from heat, stir in gelatin.

Leave to cool.

Using a small funnel, pour the mixture little at a time into the hole in the pastry top until it's all gone.

Place in the fridge and leave to set overnight.

Tip

This pork pie goes great with Mrs Slocombe's Cider and Sage Jelly on page 38.

Hartland
Tiddy, Teddy, Toddy Pastries!

When Mrs Slocombe raised the question of Hartland's favourite nibble amongst the local folk, and one that had been handed down through the generations, I got the 'Tiddy Pie', the 'Teddy Pasty' and the 'Toddy Pasty'.

Rather than risk getting it wrong and being hung, drawn and quartered by the natives of Hartland, I opted for the above title in the hope of covering all angles. You can please yourselves how you make this, a pie or a pasty, I'll leave it here; I'm gone!

Ingredients

- Shortcrust pastry (see my pastry method on page 125)
- 4-5 good sized spuds (peeled and sliced)
- 600ml double cream
- Salt & pepper
- Egg for glazing

Method

Arrange your pastry either in circles for a pasty or in a pie dish for a pie. Remember to keep some back for the lid and if it's a pasty you opt for, Devonians CRIMP ON THE TOP!

Arrange a layer of sliced potatoes on the pastry followed by a good dose of salt, pepper, and cream.

Repeat the process of layering, seasoning, and adding cream until the pie is full and domed in shape.

Note: you will probably use more cream if you make the pie.

Glaze the pastry with egg and bake in a moderate oven (appx 1 hour) until golden and a knife goes through with ease.

Gingerbread Montys

Willie Thorne, Joe Pasquale and Chris Pedlar aka 'Mr Slocombe' immortalised in gingerbread! I guess you can really tell when you've reached the dizzy heights of fame when some fruit loop from North Devon makes you into gingerbread. It's not quite like having your own star on the Hollywood Walk of Fame, but it's a pretty close second! I wasn't even going to feature gingerbread in my book; this came purely from me goofing around with them following 'Mr Slocombe's' TV appearance in The All New Monty with a host of celebrities bearing all to raise cancer awareness, encouraging all us boys & girls to check our 'bits' and break the taboo on talking about our nether regions. I figured it would be a good way to continue the collective efforts of all the folk involved in cancer awareness whilst having a bit of fun at the same time. Ahem... Hats off to you Willie and Joe for being good sports and letting me feature you in this and the continuation of raising awareness for the cause.

Ingredients

- 450g plain flour
- 200g caster sugar
- 250g unsalted butter or baking spread
- 5 tbs golden syrup
- 1 egg (beaten)
- 4 tsp ground ginger (I love ginger quite strong so I add 5)
- 2 tsp baking powder
- 2 tsp cinnamon
- Pinch salt
- Fondant icing for decorating

Method

Bung the flour, baking powder, spices, butter, salt, and sugar into a food processor and give it a good whiz up.

Heave in the rest of the ingredients and whiz up again.

Remove from the processor, wrap in cling film, and refrigerate for an hour; this will firm it up and make it easier to work with.

Lightly dust a surface with flour and, working with a bit of the mixture at a time, flatten onto the floured surface until you are left with a depth of 3-4mm.

Use your cookie cutters to cut to shape and place on a non-stick baking tray or one lined with greaseproof paper.

Once you have used up all the dough mix you can place your little 'Ginger Montys' in the oven for approx 15 mins on a moderate heat.

Remove when golden and allow to cool before attempting to decorate.

Life on the Veg

The following section contains ways to spruce up your veg for more interesting sides.

Fluffy Roast Potatoes

For perfect roast potatoes with a fluffy middle and little crispy bits on the outside.

Ingredients

- Potatoes (peeled)
- 2 tbsp plain flour
- Salt
- Pepper/ seasoning
- Rapeseed oil
- Water

Method

Place desired amount of potatoes into a pan of boiling water and boil hard for 5 mins.

Place a generous amount of oil in a roasting pan and place in a preheated oven 200°C fan/220°C/gas 7.

Remove potatoes from the heat and strain.

Sprinkle the flour over the potatoes in the pan, ensuring each one has a light dusting.

Increase/decrease the flour accordingly.

With the lid placed back on the pan, give it a good shake.

The idea is to rough them up a bit on the outside as these bits will crisp in the oven.

Place the potatoes into the roasting pan carefully as the oil will be quite hot.

Give a good seasoning with rock salt, pepper, onion powder and or chilli flakes.

Place in the oven and bake for 30 - 40 mins, turning halfway through.

Fennel & Poppy Seed Slaw

Ingredients

- 1 fennel, finely sliced
- 3 carrots, grated
- ¼ finely chopped red cabbage
- 3 teaspoons chopped fresh parsley
- 4 tbsp good quality mayonnaise
- Lemon juice – just a squirt
- 3-4 tbsp poppy seeds
- 2 tbsp rapeseed oil
- Cider vinegar – just a squirt
- Salt & pepper

Method

In a large mixing bowl add fennel, carrot, cabbage and 2 tsp of the parsley.

Mix well.

In a jug place the mayonnaise, oil, poppy seeds and a dash of salt and pepper.

Add a squirt of the lemon juice and cider vinegar.

Mix well.

Add the combined ingredients to the vegetables and stir well.

Place in a serving bowl and dress with the remaining fresh parsley.

Garlic Butter Green Beans

Ingredients

- 200g green beans
- 150g butter
- 4 cloves crushed garlic
- 2 teaspoons chopped fresh parsley
- Water
- Salt

Method

Bring to the boil a saucepan of lightly salted water.

Trim the green beans, if they need it, and add to the boiling water.

Boil until tender, drain and place in a dish.

Return the saucepan to the hob on a medium heat.

Add the butter to the saucepan along with the garlic and half the parsley.

Heat gently until the butter has melted.

Add the green beans back to the pan and simmer gently for 5 - 10 mins.

Place contents of the pan into a serving dish pouring all the remaining butter over the beans.

Sprinkle the remaining parsley over the top of the beans.

Cinnamon Glazed Carrots

Ingredients

- 300g chantenay carrots
- 3 tbsp rapeseed oil
- 3 tbsp brown sugar
- 1 tsp cinnamon
- Pinch of salt
- Water

Method

Wash and top the carrots, don't peel!

Place into a saucepan of salted water. You need just enough to cover the top of the carrots.

Bring to the boil and simmer for 8 - 10 mins.

In a separate saucepan gently heat the oil, sugar and cinnamon.

When the carrots are cooked, drain any remaining water.

Add the oil and sugar mix to the carrots and return to a medium heat, stirring well for 3 – 5 mins or until the oil and sugar mix has slightly caramelised.

Place into a warmed dish and serve immediately.

Cheesy, Nutty, Stuffed Sweet Pointed Peppers

Ingredients

- 2 sweet pointed peppers
- 300g soft cheese
- 2 tbsp chopped mixed nuts
- 1 red chilli (de-seeded and finely diced)
- Pepper
- Oil

Method

Slice the ends of the peppers off (don't discard though) and gently remove the seeds (they can be chucked).

In a bowl, mix soft cheese, nuts, chilli and fill a piping bag with the mix.

Gently insert the bag as far you can without splitting the pepper and fill up with the mixture.

Repeat with the remaining pepper.

Use a little of the mix left to stick the end of the pepper back in situ.

Bake in an oven on a moderate heat for appx 15 - 20 mins.

Sticky Parsnips

Ingredients

- Parsnips
- Honey
- Sesame seeds
- Oil

Method

Preheat the oven to 180°C fan/200°C/ gas 4. Peel and slice the parsnips into ½- to 1-inch slices.

Brush a baking sheet or roasting tray with the oil.

Lay the parsnip slices on the tray, arrange so they are all flat and not touching.

Using a honey drizzler or spoon add the honey randomly to cover all the parsnip slices.

Sprinkle with sesame seeds and place into the oven.

Bake for 30 mins, turning the slices over halfway through.

Red Hot Chilli Sprouts

Ingredients

- Sprouts
- Chilli Sauce (see page 45)
- Salt
- Water
- Rapeseed oil

Method

Bring to the boil a saucepan of salted water.

Add the sprouts, cook until they are al dente and drain.

Heat some oil in a frying pan and add the sprouts and a generous dollop of chilli sauce.

Fry until they are almost caramelised.

For an extra charred finish use a chefs' blow torch.

Tomato & Basil Salad

I, for one, cannot resist the aroma of fresh basil; teamed with colourful tomatoes, it's the perfect combination. One simple rule I always adhere to when it comes to tomatoes is I never put them in the fridge and, if you buy them from a shop, go for vine ripened ones.

If you're growing your own, I've probably just told my grandma how to suck eggs!

These are great as a light lunch or mid-afternoon snack served with seeded bread or as a simple side with your main meal.

They do go hand-in-hand with chicken piri-piri too.

Ingredients

- Tomatoes
- Basil (good sized bunch, roughly chopped)
- ¼ cup walnut oil
- 1 garlic clove (grated)
- 1 tbsp balsamic vinegar

Method

Nice and simple: heave the tomatoes in a suitable bowl.

Mix the oil, garlic and vinegar together and pour over the tomatoes.

Tip

Use variable colours, sizes, and types, of tomatoes: sliced, quartered, halved, and whole.

Grape & Fig Salad

Wow, a feast for the eyes as well as the belly! All the colour from the fruits and green stuff, the crunch from the croutons, and creamy crumbly feta cheese all blending in effortless harmony, topped off with a sticky sweet zing from the dressing.

This is great, if you have a meat-free day, served with hasselback potatoes and red slaw for an evening meal or equally great for a light lunch with seeded bread.

Here's what you need!

Ingredients

- Grapes (mixed colours, halved, whole)
- Figs (some halved, some quartered)
- Handful spinach
- Handful wild rocket
- 1 cup feta cheese (cubed)
- ½ cup of croutons

Dressing

- ¼ - ½ cup golden syrup
- 2 tsp coarse grain mustard
- 1 tbsp cider vinegar

Method

Arrange spinach and rocket at the bottom of the dish and around the sides.

Gradually fill in the centre of the dish with the cheese, grapes and croutons, topping off with the figs.

Dressing

Combine syrup, mustard and vinegar in a jug and use to randomly drizzle over the salad.

Who Wants to be a Bee-keeper?

Whilst we're on the subject of honey...

Have you ever considered what it's really like to be a bee-keeper in Portugal? Here, Roo, to whom I introduced you earlier in the book, tells you how it really is! So if you're considering being a bee-keeper at any time soon or in the future, you might want to read this first!

For some, maybe, bee-keeping conjures up an idyllic notion... Working with nature, riding in the back of a pick-up with your mates through the Portuguese mountains, sun shining as you're heading out to move the swarm to pastures new...

HELLO! I'm just gonna slam dunk you here with a bit of 4x2 to bring you back to reality!

You're slow roasting in the intense heat in the middle of the night whilst being bounced around in the back of an old transit van heading to a location somewhere in the wilderness far from any road known to man and then, despite being trussed up like the Christmas turkey, you still manage to get stung in multiple locations!

You might think that would be enough to contend with but, because you've made the bees angry, they have entered the vehicle so you have to drive in full bee-keeper's attire (not easy).

Couple that with the farmer seeing 'suspicious' activity in the middle of the night on his land and reporting it to the police, who in turn set up a roadblock to stop you (the robbers of your own apiaries!). So they're stood there in front of you brandishing guns whilst you struggle to get out of the van in all your gear looking like you've just landed from Planet Thork! The police, initially wondering what hell was stood in front of them and eventually laughing at your plight, let you go on.

Add to that being stung so badly on the face it requires a trip to A&E. You phone a family member, your mother-in-law, to come and pick you up from the hospital entrance but your face is so swollen and disfigured that when she approaches in her car and you step out to make yourself visible, she avoids you and promptly floors it to get away from you!

When Roo finally caught up with his mother-in-law (after an age of wandering around looking for her in agony and exhausted) inside the hospital and he saw the horror on her face she explained her speedy exit. "It's because you are barely recognisable and I had mistaken you for some lout who was about to carjack me!"

Roo now has to carry an EpiPen and avoids getting lifts from his mother-in-law! So, the next time you pick up that jar of honey off the shop shelf, think of the likes of Roo and Co!

Pooch & Pussy Treats

My pooches often get treats and they do love liver cake, so I thought it only right we include a recipe for them too!

Here, the founder of K9 Focus (Lynne Hall) has given me her version of liver cake.

An absolute winner all round…

Be prepared for the stampede of pooches & pussies though…

Poor Lynne; never a dull moment with rescue!

"Mum, just heave the ingredients in
the bowl, I'll supervise while she stirs.
Honestly, it's like you don't trust us!"

Lickin' Lips Liver Cake

Ingredients

- 500g liver
- 500g plain flour
- 3 large eggs
- Milk
- Requires a food processor

Method

Set oven to 170°C fan/190°C/gas 5.

Roughly chop liver (this makes it easier on your food processor), place in processor and whiz it up.

In a large bowl, heave in the flour and add liver. Mix well.

Break eggs into a jug, add an equal measure of milk, and beat.

Add to flour and liver. Mix well.

Place the mixture into a lined 2lb loaf tin.

Bake for 60 - 75 minutes until browned and cooked all the way through.

It will sound hollow like a loaf when done and your dogs will be sitting waiting at the cooker!

Leave to cool in the tin, making sure it's out of reach of those waiting licking lips!

Once cooled, slice and cut into chunks suitable to the size of your woof.

You can slice the whole loaf - chop up a couple of slices to keep in the fridge and wrap the other

As you can see, I like to serve it with a nice garnish for my pampered pooches.

individual slices in tin foil for freezing.

It will keep for up to 5 days in the fridge but freezes brilliantly.

Sadly, it does smell pretty awful when cooking but worth it to see the love in your pooch's eyes!

Just get a slice or two out of the freezer each morning and chop into pieces as needed.

Careful though, as it is quite rich so only a few pieces each day however much your furry friend begs!

About K9 Focus

For more information about the wonderful work that K9 Focus do, or to make a donation, here's their website address.

k9focus.co.uk

Note: you can't click on it. This is a book.

Picture by Mel at Mole's Art www.molesart.com

Bull at a Gate

You may have assumed that the title of this book was just chosen as an amusing reference to Mrs Slocombe's general approach to life, but there's a little more to it than that, read on...

So, there I am one day, wandering around the cows, having a count up, checking all is OK in their 'moo world' and having a chat with the ones that are about to calve down...

I'm aware the new bull is at the bottom of the field; he's young and on new territory so I'm watching him out the corner of my eye...

As I'm stood there having a chat with 'Scratchy' and big moo cuddles, I heard a high-pitched bawling coming from the direction of the bull...

OK, he's obviously not happy with my presence! Head down, pawing the ground looking straight at me! Crap!

'Slocombe, you have a problem' immediately enters my mind. Not wanting to turn my back on the beast and just leg it, I start very slowly walking backwards in the direction of the gate (the cow I was talking to coming with me) and my parked pick-up on the other side of the road.

I find myself saying out loud, "It's OK Mr Bull...Nice bull...I'm going now Mr Bull..."

Yeah damn right you are, he must've thought!

What on earth made me think I could just discreetly leave that field without a fuss? Who the heck was I trying to kid? Certainly not him!

So with over half a ton of bawling, territorial attitude thundering up the field coming straight at me, I thought now might be a good time to up my pace! Spinning on my heels, the herd instinctively parting to allow an escape path for me, I'm sure I must have resembled a stag taking off. It felt like my body left before my head!

I'm running like hell towards the gate... Closer, closer, the gate's in my grasp, I'm saying to myself, "C'mon Slocombe you got this," as I reach a speed Usain Bolt would have been proud of. My leap over the gate was going to be very quick, clean and done in one fluid motion...

NOT! Cumbersomely I crash into the gate, winding myself in the process, whilst cursing/urging my, by now, jelly-like legs to work to get me over the damn thing as the bull is only a matter of feet away!

Somehow I got over it but lost my footing as I landed. I stumbled and fell a few steps into the country road, straight into the path of an oncoming cyclist who had to act quickly and perform an emergency stop coupled with an added swerve in front of my collapsed mass...

I could see from the somewhat bewildered, bemused expression on his face that I ought to offer some kind of an explanation to my near destructive landing in front of his bicycle.

I just about managed to wheeze out the word, 'bull', whilst pointing at the gate towards him...

The little git! Stood there chewing his cud, one eyebrow raised, like butter wouldn't melt...

Bullocks!!!

Now this is done, it's on to the next crazy chapter.

Recipes Included in this Book

Melt in the Mouth Shortcrust Pastry   125

Milton Damerel Pork Pie   130

Nettle Tea   19

Nut Crusted Rack of Lamb with Herb Relish   92

Old Fashioned Rock Cakes   119

Oriental Style Salad   59

Pheasant, Bacon, Chestnut and Cherry Pie   96

Pickled Sweet Chilli Beets   46

Poppy & Sesame Crusted Tuna Steaks   103

Proper Pickled Onions   43

Red Hot Chilli Sprouts   143

Rice Pudding (The Easy Way)   113

Rice Pudding (The Traditional Way)   114

Ring Ripper - Sweet Chilli Relish   45

River Taw   28

Roasted Apple & Smoked Bacon Wraps   72

Roasted Belly Pork Slices   68

Roasted Garlic, Herb & Lemon Chicken   73

Salmon Gateau   106

Salted Beef   78

Scotch Eggs   71

Shortbread   124

Shredded Crispy Beef   62

Simon Dawson's Beer Bread   34

Sloe Gin   17

Soused Mackerel   101

Sous Vide Beef Joints   84

South Molten   118

Spit Roasted Chicken   77

Spit Roasted Lamb   86

Sticky Glazed Haddock   104

Sticky Parsnips   142

Sweet Chilli Beef Con Carne   8

Tea Leaf Reading   120

Tennessee Caramelised Burger   54

Teriyaki Glazed Ribs   58

Tomato & Apple Chutney   47

Tomato & Basil Salad   144

Watermelon, Raspberry & Vodka Smoothie   32

About the Author

Mrs Slocombe is passionate about how our food is produced and knowing where it comes from and with so many pressures on modern day food production she is a great lover of many of the traditional ways and traditional animals which were developed to suit these farming practices.

Having had her own herd of beef suckler cows she is fully versed on the benefits of slow growing traditional beef breeds which have only been fed on a natural mix of plants and grasses which grow in traditional permanent pasture fields.

This is reflected in the quality of the meat which she used in her recipes when she first set up a catering business in conjunction with producing her own beef.

With deep roots in a country background and a family of farmhouse cooks she has always loved to cook, with many fond memories of helping her Nan prepare and cook food, much of it grown on their own vegetable plot.

Mrs Slocombe loves to share her knowledge and has some great memories of time spent with the Devon Youth Service cooking with young people.

"You are your own best cook," she says and as you gain confidence and learn to experiment you can knock out some fabulous cuisine at home with some basic ingredients at a fraction of what it would cost in a pub or restaurant.

What is most important is that you cook it the way YOU like it and without all the artificial colours and preservatives of shop bought ready meals and fast foods!

Mrs Slocombe is a big supporter of a lifestyle centred on being food proud, food aware, and shopping local.

She says, "Get to know your local butcher, greengrocer, cheese shop, and fishmonger; and whilst some things like meat may work out a little more expensive the quality is better, and it will be balanced out with cheaper fruit and veg and home cooked quality food."

Food is what makes us human and, by taking a holistic approach to food, farming and the environment, we can have healthier food, do more for the environment and enjoy better food in a convivial atmosphere.

It was with all this in mind that Mrs Slocombe decided one day she wanted to write a cookery book which has proved to be another journey and learning curve in the process!

Bibliography

As you will have noticed, some of the recipes included in this book have been kindly handed over to Mrs Slocombe *with hardly any arm twisting involved.* It would be remiss not to mention that some of those contributors have also written books which may potentially be of interest to you.

Simon Dawson

Came to North Devon at the turn of the millennium and bought a smallholding with a view to becoming self-sufficient.

After many trials and tribulations, he has more-or-less achieved that goal while also writing a number of excellent books along the way.

The Self-Sufficiency Bible - Watkins Publishing 2012

Pigs in Clover - Orion 2015

The Sty's the Limit - Orion 2015

Make Your Own Butter - Robinson 2019

The Boy Without Love and the Farm that Saved Him - Mirror Books 2019

Oliver Tooley

Apart from being a writer and once radio presenter, Oliver set up Blue Poppy Publishing in 2016 (see next section).

Initially he only did this to give his own books a degree of respectability but he soon decided to offer the imprint to other authors and has now had the privilege of publishing numerous books by other Devon writers.

His own books include a fantasy series set in Iron Age Europe, and a children's series about a cat detective/secret agent named Felix Whiter.

Johnny Kingdom

Arguably one of the most loved and respected characters in the county and a man who had Exmoor running through his veins.

Johnny's passing was a dark day for many in North Devon but he left behind him an enduring legacy and memories of many a fascinating story.

A Wild Life on Exmoor - Bantam Press 2006

Bambi and Me – Corgi 2009

West Country Tales – Corgi 2012

Blue Poppy Publishing

Reviews – a sincere request from the publisher

We sincerely hope you have got, and will continue to get, pleasure from this book, either from reading Mrs Slocombe's crazy tales, or from trying out some of the recipes, or perhaps just from looking at the pictures.

If you did; please tell your friends, blog about it, review it online, or just write to us and tell us what you liked.

We always love to hear from readers whether it be praise or constructive criticism. Thank you. ♥

Oh, and don't be a stranger on social media.

Twitter

@SlocombeMrs

@BluePopyPub

Instagram

miss_slocombe

Other books

This is the bit where we suggest other books you might like from Blue Poppy Publishing.

As this is the very first cookery book we have ever published, here are a couple of our most popular novels.

A Breath of Moonscent

A lyrical memoir of a boy growing up in North Devon during and just after World War II.

The book is championed by local author Liz Shakespeare who heaps praise on it in her foreword.

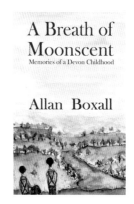

Barefoot on the Cobbles

Based on real events which took place in Clovelly in the years preceding and just after the Great War, this meticulously researched novel is a gripping read from beginning to end. Local historian Janet Few has proved her mettle in fiction writing although her research was so detailed she scarcely had to make anything up.